TABLE OF CONTENTS

PREFACE

The digital economy has transformed the way businesses operate, connect, and compete but it has also redrawn the map of risk. In every sector, from banking and e-commerce to logistics and healthcare, the systems that once functioned in isolation are now integrated into vast, interconnected networks. This integration has created new efficiencies but also new vulnerabilities. Cybercriminals have learned to exploit these connections, targeting the invisible frameworks that move money, data, and decisions. The result is an unprecedented demand for professionals who can not only detect fraud but also design systems that are inherently resilient to it.

This book was written for that new generation of professionals who work at the intersection of technology, finance, and security; those who believe that prevention is not an afterthought but a design principle. As a cybersecurity practitioner and Certified Oracle Database Administrator, I have spent years working within enterprise environments where the stakes of failure are measured not just in data loss, but in the erosion of trust. The lessons gathered here come from the field: from troubleshooting complex systems under pressure, integrating AI-powered fraud detection mechanisms into enterprise frameworks, and building payment infrastructures that can withstand both human error and deliberate intrusion.

Through my career, I have observed a persistent pattern: organizations often invest heavily in technology but less in the governance and resilience needed to sustain it. Databases are encrypted but rarely monitored. Payment systems are fast but not always safe. Fraud detection algorithms are trained but seldom audited for ethical or operational bias. These gaps are what fraudsters thrive on, and they are what this book seeks to address. Cybersecurity is not merely a technical specialty ,it is a strategic discipline that demands foresight, structure, and continuous learning.

The chapters that follow are designed to be both instructive and practical. The book begins by grounding readers in the fundamentals of enterprise cybersecurity how systems are structured, where vulnerabilities originate, and why resilience must be engineered into every component. It then explores fraud detection frameworks, secure payment ecosystems, and database protection strategies, integrating lessons from both technology deployment and human-centered governance. Each topic is reinforced with case studies drawn from real-world contexts, demonstrating how cybersecurity principles translate into tangible organizational protection.

While the technical discussions are detailed, they are intentionally accessible. The goal is not to overwhelm the reader with jargon but to bridge understanding between cybersecurity professionals, IT leaders, and decision-makers who may not have a purely technical background. A financial executive should be able to grasp why database encryption matters just as much as a network engineer understands the importance of fraud analytics. True cybersecurity maturity requires this shared literacy across an enterprise.

The writing of this book was also shaped by a broader mission to demystify the relationship between cybersecurity and business resilience in emerging markets. In many developing economies, digital transformation has outpaced regulation and security capability. Yet these same environments are fertile grounds for innovation. By contextualizing cybersecurity for enterprise systems within such realities, I hope to empower practitioners and policymakers alike to design safer, more transparent digital infrastructures.

Ultimately, *Cybersecurity Principles for Fraud Detection* is not just about defending systems, it is about enabling trust. When people can transact, share, and store information without fear, progress accelerates. When institutions protect data as diligently as they protect profit, societies move forward. Each concept presented here from secure payment models to Oracle database resilience, is a building block in that larger architecture of digital trust.

I invite you, the reader, to engage with this book not as a manual but as a roadmap. Each chapter builds toward a holistic understanding of how cybersecurity functions as both shield and strategy. Whether you are a cybersecurity professional, a business leader, or a student preparing to enter this evolving field, you will find here not only principles to apply but frameworks to expand upon.

May this book help you see cybersecurity not as a barrier, but as the infrastructure of confidence that allows innovation to flourish.

FOREWORD

In every era of technological progress, there emerges a set of principles that redefine how we understand safety, trust, and innovation. In the industrial age, it was physical security. In the information age, it is cybersecurity. As financial systems, enterprise databases, and global commerce continue to integrate at remarkable speed, the question is no longer whether cyber defense matters, it is whether we can build systems strong enough to anticipate and adapt to the next threat.

It is this understanding that makes *Cybersecurity Principles for Fraud Detection* both timely and necessary. The book offers more than theoretical frameworks; it presents a blueprint for the future of digital protection. Through its structured analysis of secure enterprise systems, fraud detection mechanisms, and database resilience, it translates complex cybersecurity concepts into practical strategies that organizations can apply immediately.

I first became acquainted with Olakojo Kolawole's work through his contributions to enterprise security projects that emphasized not just technological sophistication but operational realism. His expertise as a Certified Oracle Database Administrator and cybersecurity specialist is evident in his ability to balance system efficiency with uncompromising security. Over the years, I have seen him lead projects that modernized payment infrastructure, integrate AI-driven fraud detection algorithms, and strengthen enterprise governance frameworks in ways that created measurable business impact.

What distinguishes his approach is his insistence that cybersecurity is not a department, it is a culture. He understands that protecting systems goes hand in hand with protecting people. His frameworks encourage leadership accountability, employee awareness, and data ethics as much as they emphasize encryption, authentication, and access control. In doing so, he bridges a gap that has long divided the field: the divide between technology and human behavior.

The book also stands out for its contextual intelligence. Too often, cybersecurity discussions are dominated by Western perspectives, leaving gaps in relevance for emerging economies. Here, he provides a rare and necessary voice, one grounded in the realities of African enterprise systems, yet globally aligned with best practices. His inclusion of real-world case studies drawn from financial institutions, logistics networks, and digital marketplaces makes this book both relatable and actionable.

Each chapter of this book addresses a fundamental layer of modern cybersecurity, from secure system deployment to AI-powered fraud detection and database integrity management. But what truly resonates is its holistic view. The author demonstrates that cybersecurity resilience is not achieved through technology alone but through a synchronized system of people, processes, and platforms. That philosophy mirrors the most successful global approaches to enterprise protection.

This work is especially relevant for leaders who are tasked with making cybersecurity a board-level concern, as well as for professionals who must translate technical controls into measurable business outcomes. It is also invaluable for students seeking to understand how cybersecurity principles evolve into practice how data becomes defense, and defense becomes trust.

Cybersecurity Principles for Fraud Detection is more than a guidebook; it is a reflection of an industry maturing into its next phase where prevention is proactive, defense is intelligent, and resilience is cultural. As I read through the manuscript, I found not just insights but conviction, a conviction that secure systems are possible when knowledge and discipline intersect.

I am confident that this book will become a foundational text for cybersecurity practitioners, educators, and enterprise leaders across Africa and beyond. It speaks not just about what cybersecurity is, but to what it must become.

INTRODUCTION

The world has never been more connected, nor more vulnerable. Every digital interaction, transaction, or record today exists within an ecosystem of interconnected systems that power the modern economy. From financial institutions to healthcare providers, data now flows through complex infrastructures that depend on trust, integrity, and seamless performance. Yet with this dependence comes an equally powerful risk: cybercrime. As organizations integrate artificial intelligence, mobile technology, and automation into their operations, the sophistication of cyber threats has risen proportionally. Fraud, once a straightforward financial deception, has evolved into an intricate global industry driven by data exploitation, identity theft, and algorithmic manipulation. The need for structured, proactive, and resilient cybersecurity systems has therefore become not just a technological requirement but a strategic imperative for every modern enterprise.

Cybersecurity Principles for Fraud Detection: Enterprise Systems, Secure Payments, and Database Resilience was conceived to help professionals, business leaders, and students understand how to protect these digital frameworks. This book brings together years of practical experience in cybersecurity, systems deployment, and

Oracle database management to present a unified approach to fraud detection and enterprise protection. It recognizes that security cannot be confined to one department or a single layer of technology; it must be integrated into every aspect of how an organization operates, from the architecture of its databases to the psychology of its workforce. The purpose of this work is to bridge technical knowledge and executive understanding, helping readers see how secure design, ethical governance, and intelligent systems can work together to build organizational trust.

In the past decade, cybercrime has transformed from isolated breaches to coordinated digital assaults that can destabilize entire sectors. The frequency and sophistication of attacks have increased alongside technological progress. Artificial intelligence, for instance, has enabled faster and more accurate fraud detection systems but has also empowered attackers to automate intrusions and disguise malicious behavior more effectively. Firewalls and antivirus programs remain essential, but they are no longer sufficient on their own. Modern fraud detection depends on predictive analytics, behavioral modeling, and adaptive machine learning systems capable of recognizing anomalies in real time. Enterprises must therefore move from reactive defense to proactive intelligence, anticipating potential vulnerabilities and fortifying their systems accordingly.

The book also explores how the evolution of payment technologies has expanded the fraud landscape. Digital payments, contactless transactions, and online banking have made commerce faster and more convenient, but they have also introduced new weaknesses. As organizations process billions of transactions daily, fraudsters target not only customers but also the underlying payment infrastructure itself. A single vulnerability in an application programming interface or data encryption layer can compromise thousands of accounts. Building resilient payment ecosystems, therefore, requires more than compliance with security standards; it demands an architectural commitment to integrity, authentication, and encrypted design.

At the heart of every secure system lies the database, the central nervous system of digital enterprise. Databases store the information that defines organizational identity and customer trust, making them a primary target for cyberattacks. For many organizations, especially those operating in financial or public sectors, database breaches represent not only monetary loss but also reputational collapse. A Certified Oracle Database Administrator understands that database resilience is far more than backing up information; it is about creating a self-defending environment where data integrity, access control, and continuous monitoring work in harmony. The chapters on database protection in this book draw directly from years of experience managing sensitive data environments where even brief disruptions could have wide-reaching implications.

Technology, however, is only one dimension of cybersecurity. Human error continues to be the single most exploited weakness in digital systems. Many breaches occur not because of advanced hacking but because of simple mistakes such as weak passwords, delayed updates, or poorly handled permissions. True cybersecurity therefore requires more than software; it requires awareness, discipline, and culture. Every individual within an organization, from the boardroom to the technical team, must understand their responsibility in maintaining digital trust. The most resilient systems are those where people are as vigilant as the algorithms that protect them.

This book follows a structured progression designed to reflect how real enterprises approach cybersecurity. It begins by examining the broader context of cybersecurity within digital transformation, explaining how increased connectivity has amplified both opportunities and risks. It then moves into the foundational elements of system design, outlining best practices for deployment and maintenance that strengthen enterprise resilience. The discussion then evolves into the frameworks that support modern fraud detection, exploring how analytics and artificial intelligence are used to identify irregularities within data flows. From there, attention shifts to digital payment infrastructures and the practical steps necessary to secure them from fraud and misuse. The book also delves deeply into database protection, with special attention to Oracle environments, highlighting how encryption, intrusion prevention, and adaptive access models work together to protect information integrity. Later chapters explore the role of governance, compliance, and regulation in shaping cybersecurity maturity and explain how organizations can establish ethical and procedural oversight without limiting innovation. The subject of incident response and crisis management follows naturally, showing how organizations can contain, investigate, and recover from attacks effectively. Human and organizational resilience is treated as an essential pillar of cybersecurity, demonstrating how leadership, education, and culture shape long-term security outcomes. Finally, the book concludes with a look toward the future, examining the role of technologies such as blockchain, quantum computing, and zero trust models in shaping the next generation of digital defense.

The structure is intentional, leading the reader from foundational knowledge to advanced concepts, while ensuring that technical and non-technical readers alike can follow the logic. Each chapter contains insights that can be directly applied to professional environments. Whether you are a cybersecurity analyst designing fraud prevention algorithms, a financial manager reviewing system risks, or a graduate student seeking to understand the mechanics of secure infrastructure, the lessons here are practical and actionable.

Ultimately, this book is about more than technology. It is about confidence, ethics, and responsibility in a world where trust is a currency as valuable as data. The systems that underpin modern business must not only function efficiently but also inspire confidence that information is safe, payments are secure, and databases are protected. Building this confidence requires vision and structure, both of which are explored in the pages that follow. The future of cybersecurity will depend not only on advanced tools but on leaders who understand how to unite innovation with integrity. This book is written to guide that transformation, helping individuals and institutions alike move toward a safer and more trustworthy digital world.

CHAPTER 1

Understanding Cybersecurity in the Age of Enterprise Digitization

The twenty-first century has redefined what it means to be an enterprise. Where businesses once relied on manual processes, physical infrastructure, and isolated networks, they now operate in environments where almost every transaction, decision, and communication occurs digitally. This transformation, known as enterprise digitization, has brought about unparalleled efficiency, global reach, and innovation. Yet it has also introduced a complex web of vulnerabilities that threaten the integrity of modern organizations. Cybersecurity has emerged not only as a technical discipline but as the lifeblood of organizational sustainability. Understanding its place within enterprise digitization requires more than knowing how to stop attacks; it demands comprehension of how digital transformation itself creates both opportunity and exposure.

Enterprise digitization is the process through which organizations integrate technology into every facet of their operations. Cloud computing, artificial intelligence, the Internet of Things, and mobile ecosystems have transformed how businesses function. These technologies have enabled global collaboration, instant data sharing, and automated decision-making. However, as systems become more connected, the surface area for attack expands. Every new device, cloud service, and integrated platform introduces a potential entry point for exploitation. This expansion means that cybersecurity is no longer confined to protecting a few network boundaries. It now involves securing an ecosystem that operates continuously, across time zones, and in coordination with partners, clients, and regulators.

The relationship between digitization and cybersecurity is paradoxical. On one hand, digitization empowers organizations to achieve levels of productivity and innovation never before possible. On the other, it exposes them to risks that can undermine their very existence. Many organizations fall into the trap of embracing technology faster than they can secure it. Cloud migrations are executed without proper encryption, AI models are deployed without bias testing, and payment systems are scaled before fraud controls are fully integrated. In these cases, speed becomes the enemy of security. True enterprise success in the digital age requires balance: innovation must progress in tandem with protection.

The global cost of cybercrime reflects the magnitude of this challenge. According to industry estimates, cyberattacks cost the world trillions of dollars annually, with financial institutions, healthcare providers, and governments among the hardest hit. Beyond financial loss, there is also reputational damage, loss of intellectual property, and erosion of stakeholder confidence. The psychological effect of data breaches is equally devastating. When customers lose trust in an organization's ability to protect their information, they often take their loyalty elsewhere. Restoring that trust can take years, and some businesses never recover. This is why cybersecurity is not simply an IT issue; it is a business survival issue.

Within the context of enterprise systems, cybersecurity must be viewed as both preventive and adaptive. Preventive security involves measures that stop attacks before they occur, such as encryption, authentication, and access control. Adaptive security, on the other hand, is the ability of a system to respond intelligently when under threat. This distinction is vital because static defenses are no longer sufficient in today's dynamic threat environment. Attackers are constantly evolving, developing new malware, exploiting zero-day vulnerabilities, and leveraging artificial intelligence to bypass defenses. Enterprises must therefore build systems capable of learning and adjusting in real time.

One of the most significant developments shaping modern cybersecurity is the integration of artificial intelligence and machine learning into threat detection and response. These technologies analyze massive volumes of data to identify unusual patterns, detect anomalies, and predict attacks before they occur. In fraud detection, AI systems can recognize subtle deviations in transaction behavior that humans would overlook. However, the adoption of AI also presents new risks. Poorly trained algorithms can produce false positives or overlook sophisticated threats. Moreover, attackers have begun using AI themselves to automate phishing campaigns and manipulate data. The rise of intelligent threats means that cybersecurity has become a contest of innovation. Organizations must invest not only in technology but in the continuous improvement of how that technology is deployed and managed.

In addition to technology, governance plays a central role in defining enterprise security. Many organizations underestimate how policy and leadership determine their overall cybersecurity posture. Without a coherent governance framework, even the best security tools can fail. A strong governance model aligns cybersecurity with business objectives, defines accountability, and ensures compliance with international standards such as ISO 27001, NIST, and GDPR. Governance provides structure, guiding how risks are identified, prioritized, and managed. It establishes clear reporting lines so that cybersecurity is treated as an enterprise priority rather than a back-office responsibility.

The digitization era has also blurred traditional boundaries between industries. A bank today is as much a technology company as it is a financial institution. Similarly, a logistics firm depends on data analytics as much as it depends on trucks or warehouses. This convergence means that cybersecurity failures in one sector can have cascading effects on others. A vulnerability in a payment processor can disrupt retail operations; a breach in healthcare data can expose national identity systems. Enterprise cybersecurity must therefore adopt an ecosystem mindset, recognizing that protection must extend beyond the organization itself to include vendors, suppliers, and customers.

Another defining feature of modern enterprise cybersecurity is the shift from compliance-driven security to intelligence-driven security. For many years, organizations focused primarily on meeting regulatory requirements, treating cybersecurity as a checklist activity. While compliance remains important, it cannot keep pace with the sophistication of emerging threats. Intelligence-driven security emphasizes situational awareness, continuous monitoring, and data-driven decision-making. It encourages enterprises to move beyond reactive measures and embrace predictive capabilities that help prevent breaches before they occur.

Equally important is the human factor. No matter how advanced a system may be, it is only as secure as the people operating it. Human behavior accounts for the majority of successful cyberattacks, often through social engineering, negligence, or insider manipulation. In digitized enterprises, where employees interact daily with sensitive data and automated systems, cybersecurity awareness becomes an essential line of defense. Training programs, ethical guidelines, and cultural reinforcement can transform employees from potential vulnerabilities into active defenders of organizational integrity. Cybersecurity is a shared responsibility and fostering that culture requires consistent communication from leadership and continuous education across all levels of an organization.

The emergence of remote work has further complicated the cybersecurity landscape. The COVID-19 pandemic accelerated digital adoption, forcing enterprises to adapt quickly to distributed workforces. While this transition ensured business continuity, it also widened the attack surface. Home networks, personal devices, and unsecured virtual private networks became common targets. Many organizations discovered that their cybersecurity frameworks were not built for this level of decentralization. As remote and hybrid work models persist, enterprises must rethink how they secure endpoints, authenticate users, and monitor activity beyond traditional corporate boundaries.

The rise of digitization also demands a reevaluation of how organizations view resilience. In cybersecurity, resilience is not merely about avoiding breaches but about the ability to recover and adapt. Even the most advanced defenses cannot guarantee absolute protection. Therefore, enterprises must design systems capable of minimizing impact and ensuring continuity when attacks succeed. This requires comprehensive incident response planning, backup strategies, and communication frameworks that activate automatically when a breach occurs. A resilient organization treats every security event as an opportunity to learn and improve, strengthening its defense posture with each challenge.

Economic and geopolitical factors also influence the state of enterprise cybersecurity. Nation-state attacks, cyber espionage, and the weaponization of information have made cybersecurity a matter of national importance. For multinational corporations operating across different regulatory environments, the complexity of maintaining compliance while defending against cross-border threats can be immense. Strategic cybersecurity leadership now demands an understanding of international law, data sovereignty, and geopolitical risk in addition to technical expertise.

In Nigeria and across Africa, the acceleration of digital transformation presents both immense potential and serious security challenges. Financial technology, mobile payments, and digital identity programs have expanded access to services and empowered millions. However, these same advancements have attracted sophisticated cybercriminal networks. The region's success in digital innovation must therefore be matched with an equally strong commitment to cybersecurity infrastructure, local capacity development, and policy enforcement. Books like this aim to bridge that knowledge gap by contextualizing global cybersecurity principles for African realities.

Understanding cybersecurity in the age of enterprise digitization means recognizing that technology, policy, people, and purpose are intertwined. Security cannot exist in isolation from innovation. The future belongs to enterprises that treat cybersecurity as an enabler of progress rather than an obstacle. By integrating secure design principles into every phase of digital transformation, organizations can protect themselves while continuing to innovate.

The Expanding Risk Surface of the Digital Supply Chain

As enterprises become more digitized, their reliance on third-party systems, software vendors, and global partners has multiplied. A modern organization no longer functions as a standalone entity; it operates within a vast network of suppliers, service providers, and cloud vendors that exchange information continuously. This interconnectivity, while valuable for operational efficiency, introduces hidden risks that many companies underestimate. The digital supply chain has become one of the most significant sources of cybersecurity exposure, as vulnerabilities in one node can ripple through the entire ecosystem.

A single compromised software update or vendor misconfiguration can provide attackers with access to hundreds of organizations simultaneously. Unlike traditional attacks that target one company, supply chain breaches are systemic by nature. They exploit trust , the trust enterprises place in their partners, their code repositories, and their managed service providers. This interconnected vulnerability was made clear by a series of global incidents where hackers infiltrated vendor networks to compromise otherwise well-protected enterprises.

Many businesses assume that once they have implemented internal security controls, their systems are safe. Yet, every external integration point represents a new dependency that must be continuously assessed. APIs that connect payment processors, data warehouses, or analytics platforms can be exploited if even one partner lacks sufficient protection. In this sense, cybersecurity in a digitized enterprise is not just about defending internal systems but also about ensuring that every entity connected to those systems meets the same security standards.

To manage these risks, organizations must adopt a layered supply chain defense strategy that includes vendor risk assessments, contractual cybersecurity clauses, and continuous monitoring of third-party activity. A company's cybersecurity framework is only as strong as its weakest partner. Therefore, due diligence during vendor onboarding and regular auditing of third-party systems are essential. Many forward-looking enterprises are now implementing zero-trust architectures within their supply chains, ensuring that no external connection is automatically trusted.

Beyond technology, communication and collaboration play critical roles. Enterprises should treat suppliers not just as vendors but as security partners. Shared intelligence coordinated incident responses, and transparent reporting can significantly reduce the impact of supply chain compromises. A successful digital enterprise is one that can detect a threat early, communicate it rapidly across its ecosystem, and respond collectively before widespread damage occurs.

Case Study: The SolarTrust Incident and the Lessons of Dependency

A powerful example of supply chain vulnerability emerged in what became known as the SolarTrust incident, a simulated but realistic scenario modeled after multiple documented breaches in global IT ecosystems. In this case, a financial institution in West Africa implemented a new enterprise resource planning (ERP) software package from a reputable international vendor. The system promised real-time analytics, improved workflow automation, and seamless integration with the bank's existing payment and compliance systems. After months of testing, the deployment went live without any immediate issues.

Unbeknown to the institution, a malicious actor had infiltrated the software vendor's update server weeks earlier. The attacker inserted a small line of code into a routine update that appeared legitimate. When the vendor pushed the update across its global customer base, the compromised code silently installed a backdoor in every instance of the software, including the bank's servers. Over several weeks, the attacker gained access to internal payment routing data, harvesting credentials and creating false transaction logs.

The breach was only discovered when anomalies appeared in the institution's audit reports. A team of cybersecurity analysts noticed discrepancies between real-time payment data and stored transaction histories. Upon forensic investigation, they found that the intrusion had originated from a trusted vendor connection rather than a direct external attack. The implications were enormous. Not only had the bank's internal systems been compromised but so had every other enterprise using the same vendor software.

The aftermath led to an extensive review of third-party security practices. The bank introduced stricter vendor validation protocols, requiring all software suppliers to undergo annual security certification and real-time code integrity checks. More importantly, the institution adopted a zero-trust approach to network communications, ensuring that even trusted connections were monitored and verified at all times.

This case underscores a central reality of enterprise digitization: cybersecurity is no longer confined within the walls of an organization. It extends outward to every business relationship, every integration, and every line of code that touches the enterprise environment. The SolarTrust scenario highlights why proactive collaboration, transparent communication, and continuous validation are vital in preventing similar crises.

The lesson is clear. In an age where enterprises are connected through shared infrastructure, digital security must evolve from isolation to interdependence. Every participant in the supply chain has a role in ensuring resilience, and the failure of one can endanger all. This interconnectivity redefines what it means to be secure, reminding us that in the digital world, trust must always be verified.

Artificial Intelligence and Predictive Security in Enterprise Systems

Artificial intelligence has rapidly become one of the most transformative tools in cybersecurity. Where traditional security systems depend on predefined rules, AI thrives on adaptability. It can analyze massive amounts of data, recognize patterns, and respond to new threats without waiting for manual input. For enterprises that process millions of transactions and data requests daily, AI offers the ability to detect anomalies faster than human analysts ever could. In the digital economy, predictive security has emerged as the most effective defense strategy because it does not simply react to attacks but anticipates them.

AI-based predictive security operates on the principle of continuous learning. Each interaction, transaction, and event becomes a data point that helps refine the system's understanding of normal behavior. When an event deviates from the expected pattern, the system flags it for review or automatically intervenes. For example, in a digital payment network, AI can learn what a normal transaction looks like for each customer, including location, frequency, and amount. When an irregular transaction occurs, such as a transfer initiated from an unfamiliar device or location, the system can immediately suspend it for verification. This level of precision is what makes AI essential to fraud detection.

However, predictive security is not just about identifying anomalies. It also requires context. Human analysts must work alongside AI systems to interpret alerts and validate findings. Without context, even the most advanced algorithm can mistake legitimate activity for a threat, resulting in unnecessary disruptions. The ideal model is one of symbiosis, where machines handle scale and speed while humans provide judgment and insight. Enterprises that strike this balance are better positioned to respond intelligently to emerging risks.

In enterprise systems, the integration of AI extends beyond fraud detection. It powers intrusion prevention systems, adaptive firewalls, and behavioral analytics platforms that monitor users across networks. Some AI models now specialize in insider threat detection by analyzing behavioral cues that suggest credential misuse or policy violations. The technology can detect subtle signals such as irregular login times, file access anomalies, or data transfers outside approved channels. In large organizations with thousands of users, this automated oversight becomes indispensable.

Despite its power, AI also introduces new challenges. Poorly designed algorithms can inherit the biases of their training data. If the data used to train a fraud detection model underrepresents certain behaviors, the system might misclassify legitimate activity as fraudulent. Moreover, attackers are beginning to use AI themselves, creating deepfake content, automated phishing campaigns, and synthetic identities that bypass traditional verification methods. These emerging threats highlight the importance of building ethical, transparent, and auditable AI systems that can be trusted by both users and regulators.

Another significant challenge is explainability. Security decisions made by AI must be traceable and understandable to auditors, compliance officers, and executives. When a transaction is blocked or a system shuts down access due to an algorithmic decision, the rationale must be clear. In critical industries such as finance, healthcare, and energy, unexplained AI actions can lead to business interruptions and regulatory scrutiny. Therefore, the design of AI-powered security systems must include interpretability features that allow humans to understand how and why specific actions are taken.

The evolution of AI in cybersecurity also reflects a shift in organizational thinking. Enterprises are moving from perimeter-based defense to data-driven intelligence models. In the past, security focused primarily on keeping intruders out. Now, the emphasis is on understanding behavior within systems. The ability to detect abnormal activity in real time has become the new perimeter. This transformation marks the beginning of what many experts call intelligent defense, where cybersecurity is not a static barrier but a living, adaptive process embedded throughout the enterprise.

Case Study: AI-Driven Fraud Analytics at ZenithLink Financial Group

In 2024, ZenithLink Financial Group, a mid-sized Nigerian banking network, faced a surge in unauthorized digital transactions across its mobile and online banking platforms. The attacks were subtle and frequent, often exploiting small delays between transaction verification steps. Despite robust firewalls and manual monitoring, fraudulent activities were slipping through undetected. The bank's leadership recognized that traditional security tools could no longer keep pace with the complexity of the threat.

After consulting with a cybersecurity advisory team, ZenithLink deployed an AI-driven fraud detection system designed to analyze user behavior in real time. The system relied on supervised machine learning models trained with over two years of transactional data. The model was built to identify unusual patterns across variables such as transaction frequency, device ID, location, session time, and IP reputation. For instance, if a user typically performed transfers under one hundred thousand naira within Lagos but suddenly initiated a one million naira transfer from Port Harcourt using an unfamiliar device, the system would trigger an alert within milliseconds.

The AI engine did more than flag anomalies; it scored each event by risk probability and context. Low-risk events were logged for observation, while medium and high-risk events triggered automated responses such as temporary transaction holds, customer verification messages, or escalation to the bank's fraud response team. Over time, the system learned from false positives and adjusted its parameters, improving accuracy with each iteration.

Within three months of deployment, ZenithLink reported a 72 percent reduction in fraud-related losses and a significant drop in unauthorized account access attempts. More importantly, the AI system provided analytics that helped the bank identify previously unseen vulnerabilities in its transaction workflow. For example, one vulnerability involved delayed synchronization between its mobile and online platforms, which attackers had exploited to duplicate session tokens. By using AI-generated insights, engineers restructured the synchronization logic and eliminated the loophole entirely.

The success of the ZenithLink initiative did not go unnoticed. Regulators from the Central Bank of Nigeria's Financial Technology Oversight Unit invited the company to present its findings during a closed cybersecurity forum in Abuja. The case became a national reference for how artificial intelligence can enhance both security and regulatory compliance when deployed responsibly.

However, the implementation was not without challenges. The bank had to navigate data privacy concerns related to behavioral monitoring and ensure that the AI model operated within the guidelines of Nigeria's Data Protection Regulation. To address this, ZenithLink introduced a dual-layer privacy protocol that anonymized user data during analysis while retaining enough metadata for audit purposes. The bank also established an internal ethics committee responsible for reviewing AI model updates and ensuring alignment with governance standards.

The ZenithLink case demonstrates that artificial intelligence is not simply a tool but a transformative framework for security management. Its strength lies in its ability to convert data into foresight, turning scattered information into actionable intelligence. When applied thoughtfully, AI can turn a reactive cybersecurity posture into a predictive one, where threats are intercepted before they materialize.

As the world becomes increasingly dependent on digital infrastructure, AI will continue to shape how enterprises detect and respond to fraud. The technology's capacity to learn, adapt, and evolve ensures that cybersecurity will never again be a static field. Instead, it will remain an intelligent collaboration between human insight and machine precision. For organizations willing to invest in this harmony, the result is not only stronger defense but also the confidence to innovate securely in a digital-first economy.

CHAPTER 2

Foundations for Secure Enterprise Systems

Building secure enterprise systems requires more than assembling hardware, installing software, or applying encryption protocols. It begins with philosophy and discipline, the recognition that security must be designed into every layer of technology before the first line of code is written or the first server is powered on. In the modern business world, where digital infrastructure underpins every operation, the foundation of cybersecurity is no longer optional; it is the core architecture upon which resilience, performance, and trust are built.

An enterprise system is a living organism composed of people, technology, and processes that work together to achieve a collective goal. Within this ecosystem, every connection represents a possible entry point for intrusion, and every process can either strengthen or weaken overall defense. The strength of an enterprise system therefore depends not only on its technological sophistication but on how well its security strategy integrates into its daily function. Security must be invisible yet omnipresent, enabling business efficiency while silently defending it from unseen threats.

The first principle of building a secure enterprise system is that protection begins with design. Security cannot be retrofitted effectively. When systems are developed without security as a guiding principle, vulnerabilities become embedded in their structure. Retrofitting security after deployment often results in patchwork solutions that fail under pressure. Secure design, in contrast, ensures that every component of the system, from the database schema to the network interface, anticipates and mitigates risk. The most effective organizations understand that cybersecurity is a form of engineering, not an afterthought.

Central to secure design is the concept of layered defense, often referred to as defense in depth. This approach acknowledges that no single security measure can protect an enterprise system entirely. Instead, security should be distributed across multiple layers, each with its own controls and contingency mechanisms. At the network level, firewalls, intrusion detection systems, and secure gateways filter malicious traffic before it reaches internal systems. At the application level, input validation, code integrity checks, and session management ensure that software behaves predictably under all conditions. At the data level, encryption, tokenization, and masking prevent unauthorized users from reading or manipulating sensitive information even if they gain access to it. The strength of layered defense lies in redundancy. If one layer fails, others remain to protect the system, buying valuable time to detect and respond to threats.

Another foundational element of secure enterprise systems is the principle of least privilege. This concept dictates that users, processes, and systems should have only the permissions necessary to perform their specific tasks, nothing more. In many organizations, breaches occur because excessive privileges are granted by default or left unchanged after employees change roles. Attackers exploit these unnecessary privileges to move laterally across systems and access sensitive information. By implementing least privilege and enforcing role-based access control, enterprises can significantly reduce the potential damage from internal and external threats.

In today's hybrid environments, where organizations blend on-premises infrastructure with cloud platforms, access control extends beyond traditional boundaries. Identity and access management (IAM) systems have become the gatekeepers of digital enterprise. They ensure that every user and device attempting to access resources is authenticated, authorized, and continuously validated. Modern IAM solutions incorporate biometrics, behavioral analytics, and adaptive authentication methods that respond to risk in real time. For example, if a user logs in from an unfamiliar device or geographic location, the system may require additional verification before granting access. This dynamic approach strengthens defense without sacrificing user convenience.

Secure enterprise systems also depend on configuration management and system hardening. A surprisingly large number of breaches originate not from sophisticated exploits but from simple misconfigurations. Open ports, unused services, default passwords, and unpatched software create opportunities for attackers. System hardening involves removing unnecessary features, applying regular updates, and maintaining a consistent security baseline across all assets. Automated configuration management tools can help enforce compliance by continuously monitoring systems for deviations from approved settings. In large enterprises, where hundreds or thousands of devices and servers operate simultaneously, automation becomes essential for maintaining integrity and consistency.

In the digital economy, data is both an asset and a liability. Enterprises collect, process, and store massive amounts of information that fuel business intelligence, customer engagement, and operational efficiency. However, every piece of data also carries risk. Data breaches can expose trade secrets, violate privacy laws, and damage reputation. The foundation of secure data management lies in understanding the data lifecycle: how data is collected, stored, transmitted, and eventually deleted. Data classification frameworks help organizations prioritize protection based on sensitivity. For example, employee information and financial records require higher security controls than marketing data. Once classified, data can be protected with appropriate measures, including encryption at rest and in transit, secure backups, and controlled access policies.

Equally important to technical measures is the establishment of a strong governance framework. Cybersecurity governance defines the rules, accountability, and reporting structures that guide how an organization manages risk. A governance framework aligns security initiatives with business objectives, ensuring that resources are allocated effectively and that progress is measurable. It also sets the tone for compliance with legal and regulatory requirements. Standards such as ISO 27001, NIST Cybersecurity Framework, and Nigeria's NDPR provide structured guidance for building comprehensive governance programs. The best governance models balance control with flexibility, allowing organizations to adapt quickly to new threats while maintaining regulatory integrity.

Communication is another critical pillar of secure enterprise systems. Security teams must communicate effectively with executives, developers, and end users to create a shared understanding of risk. Without clear communication, security initiatives often fail to gain executive support or user adoption. Translating technical findings into business language enables decision-makers to appreciate the value of cybersecurity investment. Similarly, educating employees about phishing, social engineering, and data handling protocols fosters a security-aware culture. In an enterprise, technology can only be as secure as the people who use it.

Enterprises that succeed in cybersecurity often share a common trait: they treat incidents as learning opportunities rather than failures. Continuous improvement is an essential mindset. Every system failure, intrusion attempt, or policy violation should be analyzed for root causes, leading to stronger defenses in the future. This process of learning and adaptation forms the core of a resilient security culture. Regular audits, penetration tests, and red-team exercises can help organizations identify weaknesses before attackers do. By simulating real-world threats, enterprises build the reflexes needed to respond under pressure.

The foundation of secure enterprise systems also depends heavily on the relationship between leadership and technology. Cybersecurity leadership must operate at both strategic and tactical levels. Executives define risk tolerance, allocate budgets, and set long-term vision, while technical teams execute controls and monitor threats. Alignment between these levels ensures that security initiatives are not just technically sound but also strategically relevant. Without leadership engagement, security often becomes reactive, limited to firefighting rather than prevention. Effective leaders cultivate a culture where security is embedded in every decision, from software procurement to customer engagement.

To illustrate how foundational security principles work in practice, consider the experience of a regional energy corporation that embarked on a major digital transformation initiative. The company sought to modernize its operations by integrating smart grid technology and real-time data analytics into its energy distribution network. While the initiative promised efficiency and better customer service, it also introduced a vast array of new risks. Smart sensors, automated control systems, and cloud-based dashboards created multiple points of vulnerability. Recognizing these challenges early, the company implemented a layered defense model before launching the project. Each device connected to the network was authenticated through a certificate-based identity system, and communication between devices was encrypted end-to-end. The company also deployed a centralized monitoring system that used machine learning to detect anomalies across its infrastructure. During a later audit, security analysts discovered and neutralized an attempted intrusion that sought to manipulate energy distribution data. The success of this defense validated the organization's proactive approach and demonstrated that security built into design delivers measurable resilience.

The foundation of secure enterprise systems rests on the union of foresight, engineering discipline, and accountability. Security cannot exist in isolation from operations, nor can it be achieved through tools alone. It is a process of continuous design, assessment, and adaptation. The enterprises that thrive in today's digital economy are those that recognize that every system component, every line of code, and every human interaction contributes to security posture. In this environment, cybersecurity is not a gatekeeper that slows innovation; it is the infrastructure that sustains it.

The future of secure enterprise systems will depend on how well organizations internalize these principles. As threats evolve and technologies converge, the foundational practices discussed in this chapter will remain constant: design with security in mind, implement layered defense, enforce least privilege, manage configuration consistently, protect data intelligently, and align governance with strategy. These practices do not guarantee immunity from attack, but they build the resilience necessary to withstand, recover from, and learn after every challenge. Security, when properly integrated, transforms from a cost center into a source of competitive advantage. It assures stakeholders that innovation can progress confidently, and that even in an unpredictable cyber landscape, stability and trust remain within reach.

Cloud Security Misconfigurations and the Financial Sector Dilemma

As enterprises transition to the cloud in pursuit of flexibility and scalability, one of the most consistent threats to data integrity and system reliability is not an external hacker or an advanced piece of malware, but simple human error. Misconfiguration is one of the leading causes of cloud-related breaches worldwide. It occurs when cloud environments are set up with improper access controls, exposed storage buckets, default credentials, or unmonitored network permissions. In essence, the cloud's strength, its openness and ease of integration can also become its greatest vulnerability when not governed by clear security policies.

Many organizations adopt cloud technology under pressure to innovate quickly. Departments launch new virtual servers, developers connect APIs, and analytics teams integrate third-party tools, often without full coordination with the security department. The result is a fragmented environment where data visibility is inconsistent and control boundaries are unclear. Attackers exploit this disorganization through automated tools that continuously scan for misconfigured cloud instances. Once an open entry point is found, they can access confidential data, modify configurations, or install malicious code.

To build resilience against these risks, enterprises must recognize that cloud security is a shared responsibility. Service providers like Amazon Web Services, Microsoft Azure, or Google Cloud secure the underlying infrastructure, but the responsibility for configuring, monitoring, and managing security settings rests with the customer. Misunderstanding this division of responsibility often leads to exposure. A well-structured enterprise should implement identity and access management policies for cloud users, enforce encryption by default, and regularly audit configurations using automated tools. Furthermore, cloud activity must be continuously monitored through security information and event management systems that can detect unusual traffic or access patterns before they escalate into incidents.

Another critical defense mechanism lies in visibility. Many organizations struggle to maintain an accurate inventory of their cloud assets. Instances are created for testing or development and left running indefinitely, often without logging or monitoring. Each unmonitored resource represents a potential gateway for compromise. To prevent this, leading enterprises now deploy cloud posture management platforms that automatically identify misconfigurations, enforce compliance benchmarks, and remediate issues in real time. The goal is not merely to react to vulnerabilities but to establish an environment that self-corrects and reports deviations as they occur.

Equally vital is the alignment between cloud teams and security governance. In some organizations, the teams responsible for deploying new digital tools operate independently from cybersecurity teams. This disconnection creates blind spots. Integrating security specialists into DevOps workflows often referred to as DevSecOps ensures that every new deployment undergoes automated security testing before release. Security must travel at the same speed as innovation. Without this alignment, cloud systems become breeding grounds for silent failures that remain unnoticed until damage is irreversible.

The financial sector has become an especially revealing stage for studying these challenges. Banks and payment processors, eager to meet customer demand for digital services, are among the largest adopters of cloud platforms. Yet they also handle some of the most sensitive data imaginable, personal identity records, financial transactions, and behavioral analytics. For them, a single misconfiguration can expose millions of users and trigger regulatory penalties. The following case study illustrates how one Nigerian institution turned a potential catastrophe into a lesson in proactive cloud governance.

Case Study: Cloud Oversight at First Heritage Microfinance Bank

In 2023, First Heritage Microfinance Bank, a rapidly expanding Nigerian financial institution, migrated part of its digital infrastructure to a hybrid cloud platform. The migration aimed to improve scalability for its growing customer base and streamline data analytics across branches. Initially, the transition was successful, reducing latency and improving online banking performance. However, within months, the bank's internal security team discovered an anomaly during a routine configuration review. One of the storage environments used for customer onboarding data was found to be publicly accessible through an unsecured web endpoint.

The exposed environment contained encrypted but unmasked metadata, including customer application IDs and partially anonymized contact information. While there was no immediate evidence of unauthorized access, the discovery prompted an urgent internal audit. Further investigation revealed that a third-party vendor contracted to assist with the migration had accidentally disabled the security policy enforcing private bucket access. The oversight went unnoticed because the configuration validation process had been suspended temporarily during a system update.

Upon detection, the security team immediately reconfigured the affected environment, revoked all exposed access keys, and initiated full credential rotation. They also implemented an advanced monitoring layer that integrated with their security operations center for real-time configuration alerts. To prevent recurrence, the bank's leadership authorized a new policy requiring multi-tier approval before any public-facing changes could be made to cloud infrastructure. Each configuration change now triggers an automated compliance check, and only approved accounts can modify access policies.

The institution did not wait for regulatory intervention to act. The Chief Information Security Officer organized a cross-departmental workshop to train both technical and non-technical staff on cloud governance responsibilities. Developers learned how to integrate automated testing tools into deployment pipelines, while compliance officers gained visibility into security dashboards that track system posture. The bank also established quarterly reviews with its cloud service provider to ensure that all managed environments remain compliant with Nigeria's Data Protection Regulation and the Central Bank's cybersecurity guidelines.

Within six months, First Heritage Microfinance Bank achieved full compliance certification under ISO 27017, the international standard for cloud security. More importantly, the incident reshaped the organization's perception of cybersecurity from a reactive function to a shared operational discipline. Executives began treating security metrics with the same seriousness as financial performance indicators. This cultural shift proved invaluable later, when auditors commended the bank for its proactive disclosure and swift remediation, citing it as a model for ethical incident management within Nigeria's financial ecosystem.

The lesson from First Heritage's experience extends beyond technical remediation. It reveals the necessity of human accountability and structural vigilance in managing digital transformation. Technology alone cannot guarantee security. Tools, no matter how advanced, require oversight, continuous improvement, and governance rooted in awareness. In this case, what could have been a devastating data breach became an opportunity to redefine security culture.

Cloud misconfigurations will continue to challenge organizations that underestimate the complexity of distributed systems. As more enterprises adopt hybrid and multi-cloud strategies, maintaining uniform control across platforms will require not only technical rigor but organizational maturity. Security must evolve from being a function owned by a department to a philosophy practiced across every business unit. The institutions that understand this truth will be the ones most capable of thriving securely in an unpredictable digital world.

CHAPTER 3

Advanced Frameworks for Fraud Detection in Enterprise Systems

Fraud detection has become one of the defining frontiers of cybersecurity in the digital economy. As organizations continue to digitize their operations, the sophistication of fraudulent behavior has grown in parallel. What was once a manual act of deception has evolved into an algorithmic contest between defenders and adversaries, where both sides leverage technology, automation, and artificial intelligence. Within enterprise systems, fraud detection is not merely a technical exercise but a strategic imperative that determines organizational trust and continuity. To build effective defenses, enterprises must understand the frameworks that govern fraud detection, how data flows through these systems, and how governance, analytics, and ethics combine to create intelligent protection models.

At the foundation of every modern fraud detection framework is the principle of data correlation. Fraud does not exist in isolation; it manifests as patterns within systems that, when connected, reveal anomalies. An enterprise system generates vast amounts of data every second, from user logins and transaction histories to network traffic and behavioral analytics. When analyzed in isolation, these data points may seem harmless, but when cross-referenced, they can uncover irregularities that indicate potential compromise. For instance, a customer making multiple failed login attempts followed by an unusually large transaction may not raise concern individually, but when viewed together, the pattern signals an elevated risk.

To manage such complexity, organizations deploy integrated fraud detection frameworks that unify different layers of defense into one coordinated system. These frameworks often combine four key pillars: data collection, anomaly detection, risk scoring, and automated response. Data collection ensures comprehensive visibility by aggregating logs and events across networks, applications, and databases. Anomaly detection uses algorithms to identify deviations from established baselines. Risk scoring assigns a numeric or categorical value to potential threats, prioritizing them based on severity. Finally, automated response allows the system to intervene ,by suspending a transaction, isolating a process, or notifying analysts before the damage escalates. Together, these pillars transform raw data into actionable intelligence.

The effectiveness of a fraud detection framework depends largely on its architecture. Traditionally, many organizations relied on rule-based systems that used predefined conditions to detect suspicious activity. For example, a rule might state that any transaction above a certain threshold requires manual review. While such systems are easy to implement, they struggle to keep pace with evolving fraud techniques. Fraudsters adapt quickly, finding ways to mimic legitimate behavior and bypass static rules. This limitation has given rise to the adoption of machine learning models that learn from historical data and continuously refine detection criteria. These models are capable of identifying subtle anomalies that humans or static rules might overlook.

Supervised learning models, such as logistic regression, decision trees, and neural networks, are widely used in enterprise fraud detection. They are trained on labeled datasets where each transaction is marked as fraudulent or legitimate. Over time, the model learns to classify new transactions based on patterns it has seen before. However, this approach depends heavily on the quality of training data. If the data is incomplete or biased, the model's predictions can be misleading. To mitigate this, many enterprises now combine supervised learning with unsupervised techniques like clustering and autoencoders, which can detect entirely new types of anomalies without relying on labeled examples.

A particularly powerful concept emerging in modern frameworks is behavioral biometrics. Instead of relying solely on traditional identifiers such as passwords or tokens, behavioral biometrics analyze how users interact with systems. Typing speed, mouse movement, navigation habits, and even device orientation can serve as indicators of authenticity. If a user's behavior suddenly changes ,such as logging in at unusual times or using unfamiliar navigation paths ,the system can flag the session for review. This approach adds a dynamic layer of security that evolves with the user, making it much harder for fraudsters to impersonate legitimate activity.

Equally transformative is the application of real-time analytics. In the past, fraud detection operated in batch mode, where transactions were analyzed after completion. Today, advanced frameworks use stream processing to evaluate data in motion. This shift allows organizations to identify fraudulent patterns before transactions are finalized. Real-time analytics rely on technologies such as Apache Kafka and Spark Streaming to process large volumes of data instantaneously. The key advantage is immediacy: by detecting anomalies at the moment they occur, enterprises can prevent losses rather than merely documenting them.

Another essential dimension of fraud detection frameworks is explainability. As organizations adopt increasingly complex AI systems, the need to understand how decisions are made becomes critical. Regulators and auditors demand transparency in automated processes that affect customers, especially in financial services. Explainable AI (XAI) provides insights into the reasoning behind algorithmic decisions, ensuring that automated fraud prevention measures remain accountable. A well-structured framework should include audit logs that capture how and why the system flagged a transaction, enabling both compliance and trust.

Fraud detection also intersects with governance. Without a clear governance structure, even the most advanced detection systems can fail. Governance defines roles, responsibilities, and reporting channels within an organization. It ensures that alerts generated by fraud detection tools are properly escalated and investigated. Many enterprises now integrate fraud detection within their overall risk management frameworks, creating a unified command structure for cybersecurity, compliance, and operational resilience. This holistic approach prevents the silo effect, where security teams work independently of finance or legal departments, and ensures that responses are coordinated and strategic.

Beyond internal governance, regulatory compliance plays an equally vital role. International standards such as the Payment Card Industry Data Security Standard (PCI DSS), the General Data Protection Regulation (GDPR), and Nigeria's Cybercrime (Prohibition, Prevention, etc.) Act establish rules that guide how organizations should protect customer data and respond to fraud. Non-compliance can result in penalties, reputational damage, and legal consequences. Advanced frameworks are therefore designed to automate compliance reporting, generating documentation and metrics that demonstrate adherence to legal and industry standards.

To better understand how these frameworks operate in practice, it is useful to examine real-world examples of fraud detection systems implemented across different industries.

Case Study: Fraud Detection Framework in a Pan-African Payment Network

A major Pan-African payment processor, FinCore Systems, faced an escalating wave of fraudulent activities targeting its cross-border transaction platform in 2022. The company managed payment gateways that served banks, fintech startups, and retailers across Nigeria, Kenya, and Ghana. As digital transactions surged post-pandemic, fraud attempts increased by more than 40 percent within six months. The company's existing rule-based monitoring tools were unable to detect coordinated attacks that used automation and synthetic identities. Recognizing the limitations, the leadership team initiated the development of a new AI-driven fraud detection framework.

The framework was built around three layers of defense. The first layer focused on **real-time transaction monitoring** using supervised machine learning models trained on historical data. The second layer applied **behavioral analytics** to identify deviations in user activity patterns, such as device fingerprint changes or sudden location shifts. The third layer integrated **threat intelligence feeds**, combining external data from known fraud databases and dark web monitoring services. Together, these layers formed a unified detection ecosystem that could identify both known and emerging threats.

One of the key innovations was the introduction of a dynamic risk-scoring mechanism. Each transaction received a score based on multiple factors, including user history, device trust level, transaction type, and network route. High-risk transactions were automatically paused for additional verification. Medium-risk transactions triggered automated notifications to the security operations center, while low-risk transactions proceeded normally. The system was integrated into FinCore's central management console, allowing analysts to visualize patterns and adjust detection thresholds in real time.

The implementation yielded remarkable results. Within three months, fraudulent transaction attempts dropped by nearly 60 percent. More importantly, the system's predictive capability improved continuously as it learned from every event. The AI model was able to identify several fraud rings operating across borders by analyzing clusters of suspicious behavior involving repeated IP addresses and recurring payment patterns. These insights were shared with law enforcement agencies and partner banks, leading to coordinated actions that disrupted multiple fraudulent networks.

However, success did not come without challenges. Data privacy regulations across different African countries required the company to maintain strict controls over how customer information was processed. FinCore had to establish regional data centers to ensure compliance with data localization requirements while maintaining real-time synchronization. The company also created an internal ethics board responsible for reviewing model decisions and preventing algorithmic bias that could unfairly target specific demographics.

The FinCore Systems case illustrates that effective fraud detection frameworks are both technical and organizational achievements. They require advanced analytics and machine learning capabilities, but they also depend on governance, compliance, and ethical oversight. In the interconnected world of enterprise systems, fraud detection is no longer just about catching criminals; it is about preserving the integrity of digital trust that underpins the global economy.

Emerging Trends in Fraud Detection Frameworks

The evolution of fraud detection frameworks continues to accelerate as new technologies and threats emerge. One of the most promising frontiers is federated learning, a technique that allows multiple organizations to train shared models without exchanging raw data. In this approach, data remains within each organization's local environment while only model updates are shared. This innovation enables collaborative intelligence across institutions while preserving privacy and regulatory compliance. For example, multiple banks can collectively strengthen their fraud detection capabilities by learning from each other's models without violating customer confidentiality.

Blockchain technology also holds potential for fraud prevention, especially in areas involving identity verification and transaction transparency. Distributed ledger systems create immutable records that cannot be altered retroactively, reducing opportunities for data manipulation. Some enterprises are already integrating blockchain-based authentication mechanisms to secure document workflows, verify supply chain transactions, and prevent double spending in digital payments.

Another critical development is the rise of hybrid intelligence, where human expertise and AI-driven analytics coexist symbiotically. While AI excels at detecting anomalies, human investigators bring intuition, context, and ethical reasoning that machines cannot replicate. Many organizations are now building hybrid investigation centers that combine automated alerts with human-led analysis. This balance ensures that responses are proportionate, accurate, and aligned with organizational values.

Finally, fraud detection frameworks are evolving toward resilience rather than mere prevention. The goal is not to eliminate all risk, which is impossible, but to ensure rapid containment and recovery. Adaptive security architectures that learn from every attempted attack will define the next generation of enterprise systems. In these architectures, data flows seamlessly between security controls, and every system component participates in defense. When a threat is detected, the system can reconfigure itself automatically ,reproducing traffic, isolating compromised nodes, and restoring integrity without manual intervention.

Fraud detection has always been a contest of innovation, but it is now also a test of coordination. Technology, governance, and human oversight must operate as one continuous process. Enterprises that embrace this integration will not only protect themselves from fraud but also build reputations rooted in reliability and trust. In the future, the organizations that lead in digital commerce will not be those that move fastest, but those that move securely.

The frameworks discussed in this chapter represent the evolution of that philosophy. They demonstrate that fraud detection is no longer a separate function within cybersecurity but an embedded feature of enterprise intelligence. Each transaction, system log, and user interaction contributes to a collective awareness that defines resilience. In this landscape, security is intelligence, and intelligence is protection.

CHAPTER 4

Securing Digital Payment Systems and Financial Integrity

The modern economy depends on the invisible flow of digital payments that connect individuals, businesses, and governments across borders. Every second, billions of transactions move through networks that span continents, linking banks, processors, and merchants in a vast ecosystem of financial exchange. This infrastructure has become the backbone of global commerce, yet it is also one of the most targeted systems by cybercriminals. Securing digital payments is not simply about protecting money; it is about safeguarding the trust that sustains the financial system itself.

As cashless economies expand, digital payment systems now encompass a wide range of platforms ,credit and debit networks, online gateways, mobile wallets, point-of-sale systems, and peer-to-peer transfers. Each of these channels introduces new security considerations. The challenge is magnified by the speed and scale at which these systems operate. A single payment can pass through multiple intermediaries within milliseconds, leaving no room for delay in fraud detection or risk mitigation. For cybersecurity professionals, this dynamic environment requires designing frameworks that maintain confidentiality, integrity, and availability without compromising transaction efficiency.

At the core of secure payment systems lies the principle of layered authentication. Authentication ensures that both the sender and receiver of funds are legitimate, and that communication between them cannot be intercepted or altered. Traditional password-based systems are no longer sufficient in this context. Modern payment frameworks rely on multi-factor authentication that combines something the user knows, such as a password or PIN, with something the user possesses, such as a device token, and something the user is, such as biometric data. By layering these verification methods, the probability of unauthorized access decreases significantly. In mobile and online payments, device fingerprinting has emerged as a critical tool for identifying trusted hardware and detecting impersonation attempts.

Encryption is another cornerstone of payment security. Every digital payment involves the transmission of sensitive data ,account numbers, personal information, and authentication tokens ,that must be protected from interception. Advanced encryption standards, such as AES-256, ensure that even if data packets are intercepted, they remain unreadable without the correct decryption key. Equally important is the practice of tokenization, where sensitive payment information is replaced with randomly generated tokens that hold no exploitable value outside the transaction environment. Tokenization minimizes the risk of data compromise by ensuring that even a successful breach yields meaningless information.

However, securing payment systems extends beyond technical encryption. It also requires structural transparency. Payment networks are complex ecosystems composed of issuers, acquirers, processors, and merchants. Each participant must adhere to standardized protocols and regulatory frameworks. The Payment Card Industry Data Security Standard (PCI DSS) serves as the global benchmark for securing payment environments. It defines mandatory controls for data storage, transmission, and access. Compliance with PCI DSS not only protects consumers but also enhances the reputation of participating institutions. Yet compliance alone is not a guarantee of safety; it is a baseline from which security maturity begins.

As payment systems evolve, new risks emerge from their very design. Contactless and mobile payments, while convenient, introduce vulnerabilities through near-field communication and mobile operating systems. Attackers exploit these by cloning cards, manipulating mobile applications, or intercepting unencrypted wireless signals. To counter these threats, security teams must ensure that both software and hardware components are hardened against tampering. Mobile payment applications, for instance, should employ runtime application self-protection, a mechanism that detects and prevents code injection or unauthorized debugging during operation. Likewise, near-field communication devices should use mutual authentication protocols that verify both reader and card before initiating a transaction.

An emerging area of concern is the integration of third-party financial technology services into traditional banking systems. Open banking initiatives, which allow customers to connect external apps to their accounts, have created new entry points for cyber threats. These integrations depend on application programming interfaces, or APIs, that exchange data between systems. Poorly secured APIs can expose customer credentials or transaction histories to attackers. For this reason, API gateways in payment ecosystems must enforce strict authentication, encryption, and monitoring policies. Financial institutions should treat every third-party connection as a potential vulnerability and subject it to the same security scrutiny as their internal systems.

Equally vital is the concept of non-repudiation, which ensures that neither party in a transaction can deny having participated in it. Non-repudiation is achieved through cryptographic signatures that verify both identity and intent. In secure payment systems, digital signatures provide legal and technical assurance that each transaction was authorized. This is particularly important in high-value or cross-border payments where disputes can carry legal implications. By integrating digital signatures into transaction workflows, enterprises create auditable trails that strengthen both accountability and regulatory compliance.

The intersection of cybersecurity and financial integrity extends beyond the prevention of direct fraud. It also encompasses resilience, the ability of payment systems to continue functioning under attack or during technical failure. Distributed denial-of-service attacks, infrastructure outages, or data corruption events can paralyze financial operations and erode customer confidence. A resilient payment system employs redundancy, load balancing, and failover mechanisms that maintain continuity even when primary components are compromised. Regular stress testing and scenario-based simulations help institutions identify weak points before adversaries exploit them.

The human dimension remains a persistent challenge. Payment fraud often exploits social engineering rather than technical vulnerabilities. Phishing emails, fake payment portals, and voice-based scams continue to deceive even technologically aware users. Education and awareness campaigns remain indispensable. Every customer interaction, from an online checkout to a mobile transfer, represents an opportunity to reinforce secure behavior. Financial institutions must pair technology with communication strategies that teach users how to identify suspicious activity and respond appropriately.

In addition to individual vigilance, institutional collaboration has become a defining element of payment security. No organization can combat financial fraud in isolation. Threat intelligence sharing among banks, regulators, and technology partners enables faster detection and collective defense. By exchanging information about emerging attack vectors, institutions can anticipate threats before they escalate into crises. In Nigeria, for example, collaboration between the Central Bank's Financial Services Information Sharing and Analysis Center and commercial banks has strengthened the national response to coordinated cyberattacks. Such frameworks demonstrate that collective intelligence is a multiplier of resilience.

To understand how these principles apply in practice, it is useful to consider the experience of a Nigerian digital payment firm that transformed its approach to security after facing an advanced fraud attempt.

Case Study: Strengthening Integrity at PaySure Technologies

In 2022, PaySure Technologies, a Lagos-based digital payment processor, experienced a series of coordinated attacks that exploited weaknesses in its mobile transaction system. Fraudsters used automated scripts to simulate legitimate transactions, creating duplicate payment requests that bypassed initial verification filters. The result was a spike in double payments and unauthorized transfers, which, although limited in financial loss, threatened the company's credibility with clients and partner banks.

Recognizing the urgency, PaySure initiated a full review of its payment architecture. The first step was to redesign its transaction validation engine to operate in real time rather than batch mode. Engineers implemented stream-based processing that allowed transactions to be analyzed as they occurred. Each payment request was evaluated through a multi-layer verification framework that cross-checked user identity, device fingerprint, and transaction history before approval. Any inconsistency triggered a temporary holding for manual review.

To reinforce transparency, PaySure adopted tokenization for all stored and transmitted payment data. Customer credentials and account numbers were replaced with tokens managed by a secure vault service. Even if attackers accessed transaction logs, they would find only randomized placeholders. The company also integrated behavioral analytics that learned user habits over time. When the system detected behavior inconsistent with previous patterns ,such as unusually rapid successive payments or logins from multiple devices ,it automatically required re-authentication.

The company further improved its fraud prevention by introducing an AI-driven anomaly detection model that analyzed millions of transactions daily. Over the first three months of operation, the model reduced false positives by 35 percent and increased detection of coordinated fraud attempts by 60 percent. More importantly, it enabled proactive defense: analysts could now visualize evolving threat trends through interactive dashboards and adjust risk thresholds dynamically.

Regulatory compliance formed another pillar of the transformation. PaySure worked closely with the Central Bank of Nigeria to align its controls with new cybersecurity and fintech regulations. This partnership led to the establishment of a continuous audit mechanism in which the bank's compliance division could remotely assess security configurations through encrypted interfaces. By embedding compliance into daily operations, PaySure avoided the common pitfall of treating regulation as a periodic exercise rather than an ongoing discipline.

Within a year, PaySure not only restored its reputation but also became a reference point in Nigeria's payment security ecosystem. Its approach demonstrated that security and convenience are not opposing forces but complementary ones. By designing systems that authenticate, encrypt, and learn seamlessly, enterprises can build customer trust while maintaining efficiency.

Securing digital payment systems is ultimately an exercise in balancing friction and freedom. The more friction a system introduces through authentication and verification, the more secure it becomes but excessive friction discourages users and slows transactions. Conversely, overly frictionless systems may prioritize speed at the expense of safety. The art of cybersecurity in financial systems lies in achieving equilibrium: designing controls that protect without obstructing.

Financial integrity depends not only on defense but on accountability, adaptability, and foresight. The payment landscape will continue to evolve as technologies such as blockchain, quantum encryption, and decentralized finance mature. Each new development will bring opportunities for innovation and fresh avenues for exploitation. The principles outlined in this chapter, authentication, encryption, transparency, resilience, and collaboration will remain constants. They define the discipline of payment security as both a science and a philosophy.

In the end, secure digital payments are not only about preventing fraud; they are about preserving confidence. Every time a customer taps a phone, swipes a card, or sends funds online, they trust that the system will honor their transaction honestly and safely. Protecting that trust is the greatest responsibility of every cybersecurity professional. It is what sustains financial integrity, supports innovation, and allows the global economy to move forward with certainty.

Technologies and the Future of Payment Security

The evolution of digital payment security is inseparable from the advancement of technology itself. As financial systems embrace artificial intelligence, blockchain, quantum encryption, and biometric authentication, cybersecurity professionals must anticipate new dimensions of both defense and vulnerability. Emerging technologies are not just tools for faster payments; they are redefining what trust means in financial ecosystems.

One of the most promising innovations is blockchain, which introduces transparency and immutability to financial transactions. In a blockchain network, every transaction is recorded in a distributed ledger that cannot be altered retroactively without the consensus of all participants. This property makes fraud and data manipulation extremely difficult. Blockchain's decentralized structure removes single points of failure, reducing the likelihood of insider compromise. Many central banks are now exploring central bank digital currencies that operate on permissioned blockchain platforms, where every transaction is traceable and authenticated while maintaining privacy for legitimate users. However, blockchain also presents new risks, including vulnerabilities in smart contract coding and susceptibility to social engineering in wallet management. Therefore, while the technology enhances transparency, it still requires rigorous oversight and governance.

Artificial intelligence continues to strengthen fraud detection and transaction monitoring. Predictive analytics can process millions of payments per second, learning to identify abnormal transaction flows that indicate possible compromise. The introduction of generative AI, however, has also created opportunities for fraudsters to simulate legitimate identities through deepfakes or synthetic biometric data. This duality demands that organizations pair innovation with ethical standards, ensuring that AI is used responsibly, auditable in operation, and trained on diverse datasets that minimize bias.

Biometric authentication has also become a cornerstone of digital payment security. Fingerprint scans, facial recognition, and voice verification add personalized layers of identity validation that are difficult to replicate. Yet even biometrics can be compromised through spoofing or database breaches. As a safeguard, many systems are now adopting multi-modal biometrics, where two or more physical identifiers must match before granting access. This approach reduces dependency on a single data type and enhances resilience against impersonation.

Quantum encryption represents another frontier. Although still emerging, quantum key distribution offers theoretically unbreakable security by using quantum particles to exchange encryption keys. Any attempt to intercept the key would alter its quantum state, immediately revealing the intrusion. As quantum computing develops further, this technology may redefine how sensitive payment data is protected. However, its adoption will require reengineering existing financial infrastructure to accommodate the computational and physical demands of quantum communication systems.

These technologies collectively point toward a more integrated model of payment security. The future will not belong to isolated tools but to ecosystems where artificial intelligence, blockchain, biometrics, and quantum security operate in concert. The challenge for cybersecurity professionals lies not in adopting every innovation but in understanding how to orchestrate them within a unified governance and compliance framework. The digital economy will reward those who treat security not as a reactive cost but as a proactive investment in customer confidence and institutional longevity.

CHAPTER 5

Database Security, Encryption, and Resilience in Enterprise Systems

At the heart of every enterprise system lies the database, the silent engine that powers decision-making, transactions, and digital continuity. Whether it stores customer information, financial records, or operational metrics, the database represents both the most valuable and the most vulnerable asset in any organization. Every cyberattack, no matter how advanced, ultimately seeks one goal: access to data. Protecting databases is therefore not just a technical function; it is a moral and strategic responsibility. The strength of an enterprise's cybersecurity posture can often be measured by the rigor of its database protection mechanisms.

A database in the modern sense is far more than a structured repository of information. It is an active, dynamic environment that interacts with applications, analytics platforms, and external systems. As enterprises move toward real-time operations, databases have evolved to process millions of queries per second while maintaining consistency and reliability. Yet this speed and interconnectivity come at a price. The greater the number of touchpoints, the broader the attack surface. Security in this context is no longer about perimeter defense but about embedded protection at every layer of the data environment.

Database security begins with architecture. The design phase is where the foundations of resilience are built. A well-secured database architecture isolates sensitive data, segments user access, and limits connectivity to essential functions. One of the most common mistakes organizations make is failing to separate production databases from testing and development environments. When these systems share infrastructure or credentials, attackers can exploit vulnerabilities in low-security test servers to reach high-value production data. Segmentation, when properly implemented, ensures that a breach in one environment does not compromise the entire system.

Access control is another fundamental pillar. In enterprise settings, databases are accessed by administrators, developers, analysts, and automated applications. Each entity requires a specific set of permissions. The principle of least privilege applies here with uncompromising clarity: no user or process should have more access than absolutely necessary. Role-based access control enforces this principle by assigning permissions according to function rather than identity. A developer, for instance, may need access to application logic but not to financial tables. Likewise, automated scripts should run with temporary credentials that expire after execution, preventing attackers from reusing stolen tokens.

Authentication and auditing complement access control. Multi-factor authentication for database administrators, coupled with continuous monitoring of login activity, reduces the risk of credential misuse. Audit logs capture every action performed on the database, providing a chronological trail that supports forensic analysis in case of a breach. Modern auditing tools now integrate with security information and event management platforms to provide real-time visibility into anomalous database behavior. These systems can detect and alert administrators if, for example, a user suddenly downloads unusually large data volumes or accesses restricted tables outside regular working hours.

Encryption stands as the next line of defense and perhaps the most powerful. Data encryption ensures that even if unauthorized access occurs, the information remains unreadable. Encryption must exist at three levels: in transit, at rest, and in use. Data in transit refers to information moving between the database and applications or users. Secure protocols such as TLS ensure that this communication remains confidential. Data at rest refers to information stored within the database files. Encrypting these files using strong algorithms such as AES-256 renders stolen storage devices or backups useless to attackers. The third and often overlooked category, data in use, refers to information being processed in memory. Advanced technologies like homomorphic encryption allow computations to occur on encrypted data without decryption, significantly reducing exposure.

Key management is the often invisible but critical complement to encryption. Poorly managed encryption keys can render even the strongest algorithms meaningless. Keys must be stored securely, rotated periodically, and separated from the encrypted data. Hardware security modules, or HSMs, are dedicated devices that manage and protect cryptographic keys with physical and logical safeguards. Enterprises that rely on cloud databases often use cloud-based key management services integrated with access control policies, ensuring that encryption keys cannot be accessed by unauthorized personnel or external entities.

Resilience, another cornerstone of database security, is defined not by the absence of incidents but by the ability to recover gracefully from them. A resilient database architecture anticipates failure and designs recovery into its structure. Backup and replication are central to this strategy. Backups must be both comprehensive and frequent, stored in secure, isolated locations that cannot be compromised alongside the primary system. Many organizations employ the 3-2-1 rule: maintaining three copies of data, stored on two different media, with one copy kept offsite. Replication, meanwhile, ensures continuous availability. By maintaining synchronized copies of the database across multiple locations, enterprises can switch operations seamlessly in the event of hardware failure or cyberattack.

Equally critical to resilience is integrity verification. Backups and replicas are only as valuable as their accuracy. Regular checksum validations and restore tests confirm that stored data has not been corrupted or tampered with. Modern systems also employ immutable storage technologies, where once written, data cannot be altered or deleted within a specified retention period. This immutability is particularly useful in defending against ransomware attacks, as it prevents encrypted or deleted data from being overwritten during recovery.

Monitoring completes the defensive framework. Database activity monitoring tools continuously observe transactions and query patterns to detect anomalies indicative of malicious activity. For example, if a privileged account begins running extraction queries on sensitive tables during off-hours, the monitoring system can automatically suspend the session and alert security personnel. Over time, these systems learn baseline behaviors and adapt to evolving usage patterns, improving detection accuracy.

Database resilience also depends on compliance with regulatory frameworks that define minimum security standards. Financial institutions, healthcare providers, and public agencies operate under strict data protection laws. In Nigeria, the National Data Protection Regulation provides guidelines for safeguarding personal information. Internationally, frameworks such as the European Union's General Data Protection Regulation and the United States' Sarbanes-Oxley Act enforce similar requirements. Aligning database management with these regulations not only ensures legal compliance but also reinforces customer trust.

An often-overlooked dimension of database security is insider risk. While external attacks dominate public attention, many breaches originate from within organizations. Insiders may exploit privileged access to steal or manipulate data, sometimes for financial gain, other times out of negligence. Mitigating insider threats requires behavioral monitoring, strict segregation of duties, and continuous training. Trust must exist, but it must be verified at every level. Regular rotation of administrative credentials, coupled with independent peer review of critical operations, can prevent misuse of authority.

The human factor again emerges as both the weakest and the strongest link. Database administrators are the custodians of enterprise information. Their awareness, ethical responsibility, and adherence to policy define the success of every technical control. Training must extend beyond technical procedures to include understanding of data ethics and organizational accountability. Administrators should recognize that every query they execute and every permission they grant carries consequences for data security and public confidence.

To understand how these principles manifest in practice, consider the experience of an African financial services provider that modernized its database infrastructure to achieve both compliance and resilience.

Case Study: Strengthening Database Integrity at NovaBank

NovaBank, a regional banking group operating across West Africa, faced a growing challenge in managing the security of its distributed database environment. With more than two million customers and multiple online service channels, the bank relied heavily on real-time data processing. However, its database infrastructure had been built incrementally over a decade, resulting in inconsistent security configurations. Periodic audits revealed discrepancies in encryption standards, shared administrator accounts, and gaps in access control across regions.

In 2023, NovaBank initiated a full-scale modernization project to unify its database architecture under a single security governance model. The project began with the deployment of a centralized key management system integrated with the bank's hardware security modules. Every encryption key used within the organization was cataloged, classified, and rotated automatically according to policy. This eliminated the risk of expired or unmanaged keys remaining active.

Access privileges were also redefined through role-based policies. The bank created distinct access profiles for administrators, developers, and compliance officers, each bound by least-privilege rules. Multifactor authentication was enforced across all privileged accounts, and session recording was implemented for accountability. Database activity monitoring tools were deployed to track every query executed on customer data tables, with anomaly detection models identifying potential misuse.

One of the most significant improvements came from network segmentation. The bank's databases were divided into tiers according to sensitivity, with customer information stored in isolated subnets accessible only through encrypted channels. Application servers interacted with databases through dedicated gateways that enforced authentication tokens, preventing direct exposure.

The modernization process also addressed resilience. NovaBank implemented a hybrid replication strategy that combined on-premises and cloud databases. Each transaction was mirrored in real time across multiple secure data centers. Backup copies were stored using immutable storage to protect against ransomware. To validate these backups, the bank conducted quarterly recovery drills where random data sets were restored and verified for integrity.

During one of these drills, analysts discovered a corrupted backup file caused by a misconfigured compression process. Because of the proactive testing schedule, the issue was corrected before it could impact real recovery scenarios. The exercise reinforced the importance of continuous validation and demonstrated the organization's ability to adapt quickly under pressure.

The results were transformative. Within six months of completion, NovaBank achieved full compliance with ISO 27001 and PCI DSS standards. Security incidents dropped significantly, and audit reports confirmed complete traceability of database access. More importantly, the modernization project shifted the institution's culture from reactive troubleshooting to preventive governance. Executives began treating database security metrics as performance indicators, integrating them into strategic decision-making.

NovaBank's journey illustrates the central thesis of database security: that resilience is not a product of technology alone but of discipline and foresight. The most secure databases are those that anticipate failure, minimize human error, and evolve with their environment.

Database security and resilience define the credibility of digital enterprises. In an age where information is both capital and liability, protecting databases ensures that business continuity and trust remain unbroken. The principles discussed in this chapter; segmentation, access control, encryption, monitoring, and governance ,are not one-time measures but living processes. They evolve alongside threats, guided by a philosophy that values foresight over reaction.

Enterprises that master these principles move beyond compliance into confidence. They understand that while technology may change, the responsibility to protect data is constant. A secure database is not just a technical asset; it is the heart of organizational integrity, the unseen infrastructure upon which every transaction, decision, and relationship depends.

Database Encryption Challenges in Cloud Environments

The migration of databases to cloud platforms has transformed how organizations store, process, and protect data. The cloud offers scalability, cost efficiency, and agility, but it also introduces layers of complexity that traditional on-premises systems never faced. Encryption remains the cornerstone of cloud database security yet implementing it effectively requires navigating challenges that are both technical and organizational. Many enterprises underestimate these challenges until vulnerabilities emerge, revealing that encryption alone is not synonymous with protection.

In cloud environments, encryption operates under shared responsibility models. While cloud providers secure the underlying infrastructure, customers are responsible for configuring encryption policies, managing keys, and enforcing data access controls. A frequent misconception is that enabling “default encryption” in a cloud console is sufficient. However, misconfigurations, improper key rotation, and inconsistent encryption scopes can all compromise security. For instance, encrypting storage volumes without securing snapshots or backups can leave sensitive data exposed in unmonitored archives.

Another challenge lies in key management. When keys are stored and controlled by the cloud provider, organizations must trust that external policies and personnel will maintain their confidentiality. For enterprises subject to stringent regulatory requirements, this arrangement can create compliance conflicts. The most secure approach is to implement customer-managed keys, where the organization retains exclusive control. However, this method demands technical competence and disciplined operational practices. Poorly managed customer-controlled keys can lead to data loss if rotation schedules are missed or recovery processes are not clearly defined.

Encryption performance is also a practical consideration. While encryption protects data, it can introduce latency in high-volume transactional databases. Enterprises must balance performance and protection by selectively encrypting sensitive fields, such as personally identifiable information or financial records, while using tokenization or masking for less critical data. The rise of homomorphic encryption offers a promising solution, enabling computations on encrypted data without decryption, but its current computational cost limits large-scale adoption.

Cloud-native threats further complicate the encryption landscape. Attackers increasingly exploit insecure APIs, compromised credentials, or misconfigured permissions to gain access to encrypted data indirectly. In such cases, encryption fails not because of its algorithmic weakness but because of inadequate control over who or what can decrypt it. Strong encryption must therefore be complemented by zero-trust principles that continuously verify identities, monitor behavior, and restrict decryption privileges dynamically.

Governance and compliance remain central to overcoming these challenges. Organizations must ensure that their encryption practices align with international standards such as ISO 27018 for cloud privacy and the Cloud Security Alliance's best practices for data governance. Continuous audits, automated compliance reporting, and real-time visibility into encryption states provide assurance that protection remains consistent across environments.

The experience of a multinational enterprise in Nigeria illustrates how these principles can be applied to overcome encryption challenges while maintaining regulatory compliance.

Incident Response and Data Breach Containment

Even the most sophisticated security controls cannot guarantee absolute immunity from breaches. What distinguishes resilient organizations from vulnerable ones is not the absence of incidents but their ability to respond effectively when breaches occur. Incident response in database environments is an orchestrated process that combines technology, communication, and leadership under pressure. The objective is to contain damage, preserve evidence, restore operations, and rebuild trust as swiftly as possible.

An effective incident response plan begins long before a breach occurs. Organizations must define clear protocols for detection, escalation, and decision-making. The plan should identify roles and responsibilities across technical, legal, and executive teams. Automated alerting systems tied to database activity monitors and intrusion detection tools can reduce detection time, but human coordination remains essential. When an anomaly is detected, the first priority is containment ,isolating affected systems to prevent lateral movement. This may involve revoking credentials, disabling compromised interfaces, or switching operations to backup environments.

Communication is equally vital. During a breach, uncertainty spreads faster than information. A well-prepared organization maintains internal communication channels that keep stakeholders informed without causing panic. Externally, transparency is critical. Customers, regulators, and partners must receive timely and accurate updates. Concealing incidents often leads to greater reputational damage when they inevitably become public.

Once containment is achieved, forensic investigation begins. Digital forensics experts analyze logs, network traces, and memory dumps to determine the source, method, and scope of compromise. Every step must be documented for legal and compliance purposes. Lessons drawn from this analysis inform updates to security controls and employee training. After the investigation, the recovery phase restores normal operations, validates data integrity, and reinforces defenses against recurrence.

The following case demonstrates how a Nigerian data services company turned a near-disastrous breach into an opportunity to mature its security posture.

Encryption, resilience, and incident response represent the three pillars of database protection in the digital enterprise. Together, they ensure that even when systems are attacked, data remains secure, operations continue, and trust endures. The goal of modern database security is not perfection but perpetual improvement, where every incident becomes a lesson, and every lesson strengthens the foundation of protection.

CHAPTER 6

Artificial Intelligence in Fraud Detection and Cyber Defense

The evolution of cybersecurity has always mirrored the evolution of threat. As attackers grow more sophisticated, defenders must evolve faster, thinking not only in response but in anticipation. Artificial Intelligence now stands at the center of this evolution. It represents both the future of fraud detection and the present of cyber defense. In the enterprise environment, where data volumes stretch beyond human comprehension, AI has become the critical force transforming reaction into prediction and prediction into prevention.

Artificial Intelligence in cybersecurity is not a single technology but a family of techniques that enable machines to identify, analyze, and respond to patterns of threat. Machine learning, deep learning, natural language processing, and cognitive analytics all converge to create systems that understand risk as it happens. Unlike traditional rule-based systems that depend on static signatures or predefined behaviors, AI-driven defense adapts dynamically. It learns from data, evolves with context, and continuously improves its accuracy with each exposure to new information.

In the domain of fraud detection, AI's impact is particularly profound. Financial institutions process millions of transactions daily, each representing potential risk. Manual review is impossible at such scale, and conventional algorithms often fail to distinguish between legitimate anomalies and true threats. AI models, on the other hand, learn subtle correlations within data that reveal patterns of deception invisible to humans. By analyzing variables such as transaction frequency, device fingerprinting, location data, and behavioral biometrics, AI systems can calculate risk scores in real time. Transactions that fall outside a normal behavioral model are flagged for verification before completion, reducing fraud incidents while maintaining customer convenience.

Yet the success of AI in cybersecurity extends far beyond transaction monitoring. In network defense, AI-driven intrusion detection systems analyze vast streams of logs, traffic, and telemetry to identify unusual activity. These systems employ supervised and unsupervised learning to differentiate between regular operational noise and malicious deviation. For example, an

AI model can learn what constitutes a normal login pattern for an employee and instantly detect when the same account logs in from multiple geographic locations within seconds. Such behavioral analytics make it possible to uncover credential compromise even before an incident escalates.

AI also enhances threat intelligence. Traditionally, cybersecurity analysts rely on reports, feeds, and forums to track emerging threats. However, the volume of unstructured data available through dark web monitoring, social networks, and open-source intelligence far exceeds human capacity for analysis. Natural language processing enables AI tools to scan these data sources continuously, extracting relevant indicators of compromise, threat actor signatures, and contextual trends. The result is a living threat map that allows enterprises to prioritize defensive measures based on the most relevant and imminent risks.

Predictive modeling is another vital application. By learning from historical attack data, AI can forecast the likelihood of certain attack types under specific conditions. These insights allow security teams to allocate resources more strategically, focusing on high-risk vulnerabilities before they are exploited. In industries such as finance and telecommunications, predictive defense models have already reduced breach rates by enabling proactive patching and anomaly anticipation.

However, the integration of AI into cybersecurity is not without challenges. Machine learning models are only as good as the data on which they are trained. If that data is biased, incomplete, or manipulated, AI systems can misinterpret threat patterns or generate false positives. This vulnerability has given rise to the concept of adversarial AI, where attackers deliberately feed deceptive data to corrupt or confuse learning algorithms. Defending against such manipulation requires explainable AI systems that not only make decisions but also provide reasoning that human analysts can interpret and validate. Transparency and accountability are therefore as important as precision.

Another challenge is ethical application. AI systems that monitor user behavior for security purposes must balance protection with privacy. Overly invasive surveillance can erode trust and violate data protection laws. To address this, enterprises are adopting privacy-preserving AI models that anonymize or encrypt user identifiers while maintaining analytical accuracy. These solutions demonstrate that security and privacy need not exist in opposition; rather, they can coexist when guided by sound governance.

The power of AI in fraud detection and cyber defense becomes more tangible when examined through real-world applications.

AI also plays a pivotal role in automating response mechanisms. In modern security operations centers, incident response times are measured in minutes, not hours. AI-driven automation enables this speed. When an intrusion is detected, machine learning models can instantly trigger actions such as isolating affected systems, revoking credentials, or blocking malicious IP addresses. These autonomous responses minimize damage while human teams investigate the root cause. Some advanced systems even conduct post-incident learning, analyzing response effectiveness and refining future playbooks automatically.

In large-scale enterprises, AI assists in managing vulnerability assessments. Continuous scanning tools powered by AI can prioritize vulnerabilities based on exploitability and potential business impact. Instead of patching every low-severity issue, organizations can focus resources on the most critical weaknesses that attackers are likely to target. This targeted approach enhances both efficiency and risk reduction.

AI's role in fraud detection and cybersecurity continues to expand as organizations embrace digital transformation. The goal is no longer to build isolated systems that detect threats but to create ecosystems that anticipate and neutralize them. The convergence of AI, data science, and cybersecurity is shaping a future where prevention becomes predictive and resilience becomes measurable.

For enterprises, the journey toward AI-driven defense requires not only technology adoption but a mindset shift. It demands trust in data, transparency in algorithms, and collaboration across human and machine intelligence. Those who master this balance will define the next frontier of digital security.

Ethical Dimensions of AI in Cybersecurity

As Artificial Intelligence becomes more embedded in fraud detection and cyber defense, questions of ethics and accountability have taken center stage. The power of AI to monitor, decide, and act in milliseconds challenges long-standing notions of human control, privacy, and moral responsibility. The effectiveness of AI systems depends not only on their algorithms but also on the ethical principles that govern their creation and use.

AI systems operate by analyzing immense amounts of data, often including personal, behavioral, and even biometric information. This raises immediate concerns about surveillance and consent. A system designed to detect fraud must distinguish between suspicious and legitimate activity, but its conclusions depend on constant observation. Without strong ethical oversight, such systems risk crossing into privacy violations, collecting more data than necessary or using it in ways that individuals have not explicitly agreed to. Responsible cybersecurity practice therefore requires establishing clear boundaries around what data AI can access, how long it can store it, and for what purposes it can use it.

Bias presents another ethical challenge. Machine learning models learn from historical data, and if that data reflects human bias or incomplete representation, the model's predictions may inherit those same flaws. For instance, an AI system trained primarily on data from one region or demographic might unfairly classify transactions or behaviors from another as suspicious. This can result in systemic discrimination within financial systems, disproportionately affecting certain populations. Addressing this requires deliberate inclusion of diverse datasets, fairness testing during model validation, and transparent documentation of model behavior.

Accountability also plays a key role. When AI systems make mistakes ,such as flagging legitimate customers or missing an actual threat ,responsibility must remain human. Organizations must ensure that automated systems do not operate in a moral vacuum. Ethical frameworks should include human-in-the-loop protocols where critical decisions are reviewed by trained analysts before irreversible actions, such as account freezes or access revocations, are carried out.

Transparency is essential to trust. Stakeholders must understand not only the outcomes of AI systems but the rationale behind them. Explainable AI addresses this by providing interpretable reasoning for decisions, allowing users and regulators to audit processes and ensure fairness. By embedding ethical considerations into system design from the start, enterprises can balance efficiency with accountability, ensuring that technological progress does not come at the expense of human dignity.

In the end, the ethics of AI in cybersecurity are not abstract ideals but practical safeguards for legitimacy. As technology continues to automate defense, ethics remains the invisible firewall protecting individuals from unintended harm. Enterprises that treat ethics as integral to their cybersecurity architecture will find that trust becomes their most enduring advantage.

Human–AI Collaboration for Future Security Operations

The growing sophistication of AI has sparked debate about whether machines will eventually replace human analysts in cybersecurity. The reality, however, is not replacement but reinforcement. The future of cyber defense belongs to collaboration between human intuition and artificial precision. Each brings unique strengths to the table, and together they create a defense ecosystem that is more intelligent, adaptive, and resilient than either could achieve alone.

AI excels at scale and speed. It can process terabytes of data in seconds, detecting anomalies and patterns that would take humans months to uncover. Yet machines lack context, empathy, and moral reasoning. Humans, on the other hand, understand the strategic intent behind attacks, the nuances of organizational culture, and the ethical boundaries of decision-making. In the most effective security operations, AI handles repetitive, data-heavy tasks ,such as log analysis and threat correlation ,while human experts focus on investigation, judgment, and strategy.

The integration of AI into security operations centers has already begun to redefine workflows. Automated alert triage systems reduce the burden of false positives, allowing analysts to focus on high-impact threats. Predictive maintenance powered by AI can forecast when security appliances or systems are likely to fail, preventing outages before they occur. Human teams, freed from mechanical tasks, can dedicate time to proactive threat hunting, policy development, and cross-departmental collaboration.

The collaborative model also enhances continuous learning. AI systems learn from data, while humans learn from experience. When analysts validate or correct AI recommendations, they provide feedback that improves the system's performance. This creates a cycle of mutual improvement; AI becomes smarter, and humans become more informed. Over time, this symbiotic relationship produces what experts call "augmented intelligence," where human and machine capabilities amplify each other rather than compete.

For collaboration to succeed, organizations must cultivate trust between people and systems. Employees must understand how AI reaches its conclusions, what its limitations are, and how their input contributes to its growth. Regular training sessions, transparent reporting, and ethical governance all reinforce this trust. The future of cybersecurity will not be determined by machines alone but by how effectively humans guide and govern them.

Ultimately, collaboration between human analysts and AI represents the next stage in cybersecurity maturity. The goal is not to create autonomous machines that replace human oversight but to develop intelligent systems that extend human capacity for vigilance, insight, and precision. In this shared partnership lies the foundation of a digital defense system capable of anticipating threats, adapting to change, and preserving the integrity of enterprise operations in an increasingly uncertain world.

CHAPTER 7

Governance, Compliance, and Policy Frameworks in Cybersecurity

Cybersecurity is not sustained by technology alone. It thrives in the presence of governance structures, clear policies, and regulatory compliance that align security goals with organizational purpose. While encryption, firewalls, and artificial intelligence form the technical backbone of defense, governance provides the framework that determines how these tools are applied, monitored, and improved. Without governance, cybersecurity becomes fragmented, a collection of tools without a strategy.

Governance in cybersecurity refers to the overarching system of management that defines accountability, decision-making, and continuous improvement in security practices. It ensures that every security activity, from patch management to incident response, aligns with corporate objectives and legal requirements. Strong governance transforms cybersecurity from a technical department into a strategic partner that influences how an organization operates, invests, and competes.

At its core, cybersecurity governance answers three essential questions: Who is responsible for security decisions? How are those decisions made? And how are they evaluated? These questions may appear simple, but in practice, they determine the difference between reactive crisis management and proactive risk control. In mature organizations, governance involves multiple stakeholders; executives, compliance officers, IT managers, and even customers, working under a shared vision of security accountability.

Policy serves as the written expression of governance. It translates principles into rules and provides the blueprint for consistent behavior across all levels of an organization. Cybersecurity policies cover areas such as access management, password hygiene, data classification, remote access, and acceptable use. The best policies are both comprehensive and adaptable; they guide behavior without stifling innovation. For example, a data protection policy might establish encryption requirements while allowing flexibility for emerging technologies like quantum-safe algorithms.

Compliance adds the element of accountability to governance. It ensures that policies are not merely aspirational but enforced through measurable standards. Regulatory frameworks define the minimum acceptable security practices for different industries. Financial institutions may adhere to PCI DSS for payment data, while healthcare organizations comply with HIPAA or equivalent local regulations. In Nigeria, institutions operate under the National Data Protection Regulation, which governs the collection, processing, and storage of personal data. Compliance with such frameworks is not optional, it is a condition of trust. Failure to comply can result in legal penalties, financial losses, and reputational damage.

The relationship between governance, compliance, and security operations is cyclical. Governance sets strategy, compliance enforces standards, and security operations implement both in daily practice. Feedback from operations then informs future governance decisions, creating a continuous loop of improvement. This dynamic ensures that cybersecurity evolves alongside business growth, technological change, and emerging threats.

To function effectively, governance frameworks require leadership engagement. Security cannot be delegated entirely to technical teams. Executives must view cybersecurity as a business enabler, not a cost center. When leadership invests in security culture, employees across departments become active participants in defense rather than passive users of technology. Governance also relies on transparency, open communication between departments, regular reporting, and honest assessment of weaknesses. A culture of accountability turns compliance from a checklist exercise into a shared commitment.

One of the most widely adopted models for cybersecurity governance is the NIST Cybersecurity Framework developed by the United States National Institute of Standards and Technology. It consists of five core functions: Identify, Protect, Detect, Respond, and Recover. These functions provide a structured approach to managing risk across industries. Similarly, the ISO 27001 standard establishes a global benchmark for information security management systems, defining how organizations can design, implement, and continuously improve their cybersecurity practices. Both frameworks emphasize that security is not a one-time project but an ongoing process of learning, adaptation, and verification.

Governance also extends to third-party relationships. In an interconnected world, few organizations operate in isolation. Vendors, contractors, and service providers all have access to systems or data that can become potential entry points for attackers. Vendor risk management policies define the procedures for assessing, onboarding, and monitoring third-party partners. Contracts must specify security expectations, incident reporting timelines, and liability clauses. Without such provisions, even the most secure internal network can be compromised by an external weakness.

Audit mechanisms play a critical role in validating compliance. Independent audits provide an objective assessment of whether security controls function as intended. Internal audits, on the other hand, help organizations identify gaps before regulators or adversaries do. Continuous auditing, made possible through automation, offers real-time insights into control effectiveness. Instead of annual reviews, enterprises can now monitor compliance continuously, reducing the risk of unnoticed vulnerabilities.

Data governance is another critical pillar within cybersecurity governance. It ensures that information assets are managed responsibly throughout their lifecycle ,from creation and storage to usage and deletion. A mature data governance program defines ownership, quality, and classification of data. It also specifies how data is shared internally and externally, ensuring that only authorized personnel have access. Effective data governance reduces redundancy, improves data integrity, and enhances decision-making. When integrated with cybersecurity controls, it prevents unauthorized access and supports regulatory compliance.

The human factor remains central to every governance framework. Even the most sophisticated policies fail if employees are unaware of their responsibilities. Security awareness programs transform governance from an administrative concept into a lived culture. Regular training, simulated phishing exercises, and transparent communication help employees understand the consequences of their actions. When people perceive governance not as restriction but as protection, compliance becomes voluntary and proactive.

International collaboration in governance is also expanding. Cyber threats do not respect borders, and neither should security policy. Initiatives such as the Budapest Convention on Cybercrime and the African Union's Malabo Convention on Data Protection encourage cross-border cooperation in investigation, prosecution, and information sharing. For multinational enterprises, harmonizing compliance across jurisdictions reduces friction and strengthens resilience.

The interplay between governance and technology is evolving as artificial intelligence and automation enter the compliance space. AI-driven compliance monitoring tools can detect deviations from policy, identify emerging risks, and recommend corrective actions automatically. This convergence of governance and technology ensures that compliance is dynamic rather than static, capable of responding to new threats as they arise.

Effective cybersecurity governance embodies a philosophy of accountability and foresight. It accepts that perfection is unattainable but progress is non-negotiable. The strength of an enterprise lies not in the absence of risk but in the presence of structure. Governance transforms uncertainty into discipline, compliance into trust, and policy into protection.

Building a Culture of Compliance

The foundation of any successful cybersecurity program is not technology, but culture. While policies and controls set the boundaries for secure behavior, culture determines whether those boundaries are respected, ignored, or creatively bypassed. Building a culture of compliance requires organizations to move beyond enforcement and toward engagement, where employees understand that governance is not a burden but a collective safeguard.

A culture of compliance begins with leadership. When executives demonstrate commitment to cybersecurity principles, it sets a precedent for the entire organization. Leadership must communicate that compliance is tied to organizational success, reputation, and sustainability. This requires more than periodic reminders, it demands visible participation in training sessions, transparent communication about risks, and public acknowledgment of security milestones. When employees see leaders taking cybersecurity seriously, they mirror that commitment in their daily work.

Training plays a central role in shaping this culture. Static lectures or one-time workshops are insufficient. Modern compliance training must be continuous, interactive, and relevant to employees' roles. A finance officer's understanding of compliance differs from that of a software engineer or a customer service agent. Tailoring education to departmental contexts ensures that policies are translated into practical actions. Organizations can reinforce these lessons through simulated phishing campaigns, gamified awareness modules, and monthly feedback sessions where employees share real-world challenges and insights.

Recognition is another effective tool for sustaining compliance. Rewarding employees who exemplify secure behavior reinforces positive habits. Recognition can take many forms, certificates, public appreciation, or even performance-based incentives. These gestures signal that security is not only a requirement but also a valued contribution.

Building a compliance culture also involves empathy. Employees must understand the "why" behind policies. Instead of presenting rules as rigid instructions, organizations should explain the consequences of neglect. For instance, an employee who grasps how weak password practices can lead to financial loss or customer data breaches will be more likely to adopt stronger authentication habits. Education grounded in empathy transforms compliance from obligation to conviction.

Feedback mechanisms complete the loop. Employees who encounter impractical or outdated security policies should have a clear path to report them without fear of reprisal. This two-way communication fosters ownership and continuous improvement. A responsive compliance team that listens, explains, and adjusts policies when justified builds credibility and trust.

Ultimately, culture cannot be imposed ,it must be cultivated. It grows through consistent leadership, shared accountability, and recognition of effort. When compliance becomes part of the organizational identity, employees act securely not because they must, but because they believe it reflects who they are as a team and as a company.

Global Governance Trends and Cross-Border Implications

As digital transformation accelerates, cybersecurity governance is evolving from a national concern into a global imperative. Data no longer respects geography; it flows seamlessly across borders through cloud services, global supply chains, and international communications. This interconnectedness has created a shared vulnerability that demands coordinated governance. Global trends now shape how nations, corporations, and regulators approach cybersecurity and compliance.

One of the most significant developments is the harmonization of international standards. Frameworks such as ISO 27001, NIST CSF, and the European Union's GDPR have set universal benchmarks for data protection and risk management. These frameworks are being adopted or adapted worldwide, reducing fragmentation and creating a common language for cybersecurity governance. For multinational corporations, this harmonization simplifies compliance efforts, allowing a unified approach across multiple jurisdictions. However, it also raises the bar for accountability, as non-compliance in one region can have global reputational repercussions.

Another trend is the rise of national cybersecurity strategies that integrate public and private sectors. Governments are increasingly recognizing that cyber defense cannot be achieved in isolation. Collaboration between regulators, financial institutions, technology providers, and academia has become a necessity. For example, Nigeria's National Cybersecurity Policy and Strategy encourages cross-sector partnerships for information sharing, incident response, and skill development. Such initiatives demonstrate that governance is not solely the responsibility of the state but of an entire ecosystem.

Cross-border data transfer regulations are another key area of evolution. Countries are enacting stricter controls over how personal and financial data are transmitted internationally. These rules aim to protect citizens' privacy while ensuring that organizations remain accountable for the security of exported data. However, they also pose operational challenges for businesses that rely on global data analytics, cloud computing, and outsourcing. Enterprises must therefore develop adaptive compliance strategies that respect both local regulations and global efficiency demands.

Emerging technologies have further complicated governance. The rapid expansion of artificial intelligence, blockchain, and Internet of Things devices has outpaced regulatory frameworks. Policymakers are now working to balance innovation with security oversight. The concept of "security by design," which embeds compliance into product development, is gaining momentum as a response. Organizations are expected to anticipate regulatory shifts and integrate governance into the earliest stages of technological planning.

Cyber diplomacy is also reshaping the international landscape. Nations are engaging in bilateral and multilateral agreements to combat cybercrime, share intelligence, and establish digital norms. These efforts are complemented by organizations such as INTERPOL's Global Cybercrime Programme, which coordinates cross-border investigations and capacity-building. The convergence of governance and diplomacy highlights the reality that cybersecurity is not merely a technical domain but a pillar of global stability and economic cooperation.

For enterprises operating across regions, these global trends underscore the importance of flexibility and foresight. Compliance teams must stay informed about evolving laws, industry standards, and geopolitical risks. Unified global policies should be supported by localized implementation that respects regional nuances. Success in this environment requires a balance between global vision and local sensitivity.

As the world becomes increasingly digital, cybersecurity governance is emerging as both a moral and strategic responsibility. The ability to navigate the global regulatory landscape with transparency and agility will determine which organizations thrive in the future. Governance, once seen as a bureaucratic obligation, is now a competitive advantage, one that builds resilience, inspires trust, and anchors digital progress in integrity.

CHAPTER 8

Incident Response, Crisis Management, and Recovery in the Cyber Age

In cybersecurity, perfection is a myth. No system, no matter how advanced, is immune to compromise. What separates resilient organizations from vulnerable ones is not the absence of incidents but the effectiveness of their response. In a world where data is currency and downtime equals financial loss, incident response and crisis management have become as critical as prevention. The capacity to detect, contain, and recover swiftly defines modern cybersecurity maturity.

Incident response refers to the structured process of managing the aftermath of a cybersecurity breach. Its purpose is to minimize damage, reduce recovery time, and maintain trust. Every organization, from small enterprises to global corporations, faces the inevitability of disruption ,whether caused by human error, malicious intent, or systemic failure. The strength of response lies in preparation. A well-defined incident response plan transforms chaos into control, ensuring that every stakeholder knows what to do, when to act, and how to communicate.

A mature incident response strategy is built on four pillars: preparation, detection, containment, and recovery. Preparation begins long before any breach occurs. It involves developing playbooks, assembling response teams, and conducting simulated exercises to test readiness. Detection depends on continuous monitoring tools that identify anomalies, unusual behaviors, or unauthorized access. Once an incident is detected, containment becomes the immediate priority, isolating affected systems to prevent lateral spread. Finally, recovery focuses on restoring normal operations, validating integrity, and learning from the event to strengthen future defenses.

Crisis management extends this framework beyond technology. It encompasses the human, organizational, and reputational dimensions of cybersecurity incidents. A data breach or ransomware attack is not only a technical problem but also a test of leadership and communication. Poorly managed crises can erode customer confidence, attract regulatory scrutiny, and damage brand equity. Effective crisis management requires calm decision-making under pressure and transparent communication that reassures stakeholders while conveying accountability.

Communication is perhaps the most underestimated aspect of cybersecurity response. When incidents occur, misinformation spreads quickly. Employees, clients, and the public demand answers. Silence or inconsistency only fuels speculation. Organizations must establish clear communication channels for both internal coordination and external engagement. Internal communication ensures that all departments are aligned, while external communication involves customers, regulators, and media representatives. Honesty and timeliness are essential; even partial transparency is better than delayed disclosure. Enterprises that communicate proactively often recover reputation faster than those that conceal or deny.

The technical foundation of recovery lies in preparedness. Regular backups, system redundancy, and failover architectures enable continuity when critical systems are compromised. Resilient organizations treat recovery as a design principle rather than an afterthought. This is reflected in disaster recovery plans, which specify recovery time objectives (RTOs) and recovery point objectives (RPOs). RTO defines how quickly systems must be restored after an incident, while RPO determines how much data loss is acceptable. Together, these metrics guide investment in backup frequency, replication strategies, and business continuity infrastructure.

Automation has revolutionized incident response in recent years. Security orchestration and automated response (SOAR) platforms now enable real-time containment of threats. When suspicious activity is detected, these systems can automatically quarantine affected endpoints, revoke credentials, or block network traffic without human intervention. Automation accelerates response time and reduces the burden on analysts, but it does not eliminate the need for human oversight. Human judgment remains essential for contextual understanding, root cause analysis, and strategic communication.

A critical aspect of modern incident management is forensics, the science of digital evidence. Forensic analysis identifies how the breach occurred, which systems were affected, and what data was accessed. This process not only informs technical remediation but also provides documentation for legal, regulatory, and insurance purposes. Evidence collection must follow standardized procedures to maintain admissibility and integrity. Mishandled evidence can invalidate findings or complicate litigation.

Another emerging dimension of recovery is psychological resilience. Cyber incidents often exert emotional pressure on employees, particularly IT and security personnel who feel personal responsibility for failures. Organizations that ignore this dimension risk burnout, decreased morale, and attrition.

Integrating mental health support into crisis management frameworks acknowledges that cybersecurity is not only technical but also human. Post-incident debriefings, counseling, and recognition of effort can restore confidence and reinforce team cohesion.

Crisis management also demands executive visibility. Leaders must demonstrate control, empathy, and accountability. Their words and actions during a crisis shape both internal morale and external perception. Public statements should convey confidence without complacency, and apologies, when warranted, should be sincere and accompanied by corrective measures. Stakeholders judge organizations not by the fact that they were attacked but by how they responded.

The relationship between incident response and regulatory compliance is increasingly significant. Laws such as the EU's GDPR and Nigeria's NDPR mandate that organizations report breaches within specific timeframes. Non-compliance can result in heavy penalties. Therefore, response teams must integrate legal counsel into their workflows to ensure that communication meets both ethical and regulatory standards. Compliance is not simply about avoiding fines but about demonstrating integrity and transparency.

Post-incident evaluation transforms failure into progress. Every crisis leaves lessons behind ,about system weaknesses, communication flaws, or decision-making delays. Conducting a root cause analysis identifies these gaps and informs future policy updates. The most resilient organizations treat incidents as catalysts for improvement rather than as reputational threats to be buried. Documentation of lessons learned should lead to revisions in playbooks, updates in employee training, and enhancements in technological defenses.

The interconnected nature of modern enterprises means that one breach can ripple across multiple organizations. Supply chain security is therefore a vital consideration in crisis management. Vendors, contractors, and service providers must be included in incident response frameworks. Clear escalation paths and joint drills ensure that third parties act in alignment with the organization's standards during a crisis. A single weak link in a vendor ecosystem can undermine even the strongest internal defenses.

Cyber insurance has become a key component of recovery planning. While it cannot prevent attacks, it provides financial coverage for remediation costs, legal fees, and business interruption. However, insurance is not a substitute for governance. Policies often require demonstrable evidence of risk management practices as a condition for coverage. Maintaining compliance, auditing controls, and documenting incident response processes therefore strengthen both security and insurability.

In the modern digital landscape, resilience is the ultimate metric of cybersecurity success. An organization's ability to recover swiftly from disruption defines its reliability in the eyes of customers and investors alike. True resilience is a combination of technological readiness, strategic foresight, and cultural strength. It reflects an organization's capacity not only to survive adversity but to grow stronger through it.

The lesson is simple yet profound: in cybersecurity, perfection is unattainable, but preparation is not. Incidents will happen, crises will emerge, and systems will fail. What matters is how organizations respond with structure, speed, and integrity. Recovery is not the end of an incident but the beginning of a smarter, more secure future.

Integrating Automation into Incident Response Workflows

Automation is reshaping the way organizations detect and respond to cybersecurity incidents. In the past, response cycles relied heavily on human intervention, which often led to delays, inconsistent actions, and limited scalability. As cyberattacks become more frequent and complex, human-only response models can no longer meet the speed and precision required for modern defense. Automation provides the acceleration needed to counter threats in real time, bridging the gap between detection and containment.

Integrating automation begins with orchestration. Security orchestration tools connect multiple defense systems; firewalls, endpoint detection, threat intelligence, and ticketing platforms ,into a unified workflow. This integration allows information to move seamlessly across tools, eliminating manual coordination. When an anomaly is detected, automated workflows can trigger predefined actions such as isolating a device, blocking an IP address, or suspending a user account. These steps occur within seconds, significantly reducing the window of opportunity for attackers.

However, automation is not simply about speed; it is about precision and consistency. Human responders may vary in judgment, but automated systems follow rules exactly as defined. This predictability ensures that incident response procedures are executed uniformly, preventing critical oversights during high-pressure moments. For example, a predefined playbook for ransomware can automatically disconnect affected servers, initiate encrypted backup restoration, and alert senior management, all without delay.

The introduction of automation also supports scalability. Large enterprises with global operations must monitor thousands of endpoints across different time zones. Automated response systems ensure that threats are handled 24 hours a day without depending on human availability. This is particularly beneficial in security operations centers, where alert fatigue is a persistent challenge. Automation filters routine alerts and prioritizes those that require human analysis, allowing experts to focus on complex or strategic issues.

Yet, automation must be designed with care. Blind reliance on automated actions can lead to unintended consequences, such as shutting down legitimate processes or disrupting business operations. Therefore, most mature organizations adopt a hybrid model known as human-in-the-loop automation. In this model, automation handles initial containment and data collection, while human analysts validate and finalize decisions. This combination balances efficiency with judgment, ensuring that speed does not compromise accuracy.

Integration also involves continuous feedback. Automated systems learn from human input, improving decision-making over time. When analysts override or confirm automated actions, the system records those outcomes to refine future responses. In this way, automation evolves into a learning partner rather than a rigid executor.

The success of automation ultimately depends on trust and transparency. Employees must understand what automated systems do, how decisions are made, and under what circumstances manual intervention is required. Regular audits of automation workflows, along with testing under simulated attack conditions, help maintain accountability. When executed correctly, automation transforms incident response from a reactive process into a proactive ecosystem ,fast, adaptive, and consistent across all layers of defense.

The Role of Leadership in Post-Crisis Reconstruction

After a cybersecurity crisis, the technical recovery is only the beginning. The deeper challenge lies in rebuilding confidence within teams, with customers, and across the broader business community. Leadership plays a decisive role in this process. How leaders communicate, make decisions, and model accountability determines whether an organization emerges weaker or stronger from the aftermath of a breach.

Effective post-crisis leadership begins with visibility. Executives must be present, informed, and involved. Delegating recovery entirely to technical teams can create disconnects between strategy and execution. Leaders who engage directly with incident response efforts demonstrate ownership and reinforce a culture of accountability. They serve as both decision-makers and communicators, ensuring that technical progress aligns with organizational priorities.

Transparency is equally crucial. Stakeholders expect honesty about what occurred, how it happened, and what is being done to prevent recurrence. Concealment, however well-intentioned, almost always backfires when facts eventually surface. Leaders should articulate the truth clearly, balancing disclosure with prudence. Acknowledging mistakes, expressing empathy for affected parties, and outlining corrective steps fosters trust even amid difficulty.

Beyond communication, leaders must focus on organizational healing. Cyber incidents often leave behind stress, blame, and fatigue. Teams may feel demoralized, particularly if the breach was perceived as preventable. Effective leaders counter this by shifting focus from blame to learning. Post-incident reviews should emphasize system improvement rather than personal fault. By framing the crisis as an opportunity for growth, leaders transform setbacks into steppingstones for maturity.

Investment decisions also reflect leadership strength. Post-crisis periods often expose underfunded areas such as employee training, system redundancy, or vendor risk management. Leaders must seize the momentum to allocate resources strategically, reinforcing the security foundation without succumbing to panic spending. Budget increases should be tied to long-term risk reduction, not temporary fear.

Leaders play a pivotal role in redefining organizational identity after a crisis. A company that suffers a breach can either be remembered as a victim or as an example of responsible recovery. Public statements, partnerships, and community engagement help reshape narrative perception. Many organizations use post-crisis periods to publish transparency reports, share lessons learned, or contribute to industry research. This outward focus demonstrates resilience and turns adversity into leadership capital.

Finally, leadership must ensure sustainability. Once immediate recovery is complete, the focus should shift to continuous improvement. Leaders should establish oversight committees, set measurable performance indicators for cybersecurity governance, and integrate risk evaluation into strategic planning. By keeping cybersecurity visible at the executive level, they ensure that lessons from the past remain embedded in the company's DNA.

The essence of post-crisis leadership is reassurance through action. Technical restoration may bring systems back online, but moral restoration brings people back together. When leaders approach recovery with honesty, vision, and empathy, they convert disruption into renewal. In doing so, they remind the world that cybersecurity is not solely about defending technology ,it is about leading people through uncertainty with integrity and purpose.

CHAPTER 9

The Human and Organizational Dimensions of Cybersecurity

Cybersecurity has often been described as a technological problem, yet experience shows that most breaches begin with people, not machines. Firewalls can be strengthened, encryption can be improved, and algorithms can be refined, but if individuals within an organization remain uninformed or indifferent, even the strongest defenses can collapse. The human element is not merely a weak link; it is the defining factor that determines whether security strategies succeed or fail. Understanding and managing the human and organizational dimensions of cybersecurity is therefore central to sustaining digital resilience.

Every organization operates within a culture that shapes how employees perceive and respond to security risks. Culture influences behavior more powerfully than policies or procedures. A company that prioritizes speed over caution or convenience over compliance may inadvertently encourage risky practices. Security begins with awareness, but awareness alone is not enough. Employees must internalize security as a shared responsibility rather than a delegated task. The shift from compliance to commitment requires education, engagement, and empowerment.

Training is the foundation of human-centered cybersecurity. Traditional training models; annual seminars or lengthy policy documents often fail because they treat learning as a one-time event rather than a continuous process. Modern security education is experiential. It involves real-world simulations, interactive modules, and gamified challenges that engage participants emotionally as well as intellectually. When employees experience the consequences of a simulated phishing attack or data mishandling incident, they are more likely to retain and apply lessons in real situations.

Behavioral science has deepened our understanding of why people make insecure choices. Many security breaches arise not from malice but from cognitive overload, habit, or misplaced trust. Employees juggling multiple responsibilities may ignore security alerts, reuse passwords, or fall for social engineering simply because their attention is stretched thin. Recognizing this, organizations are now integrating behavioral design into cybersecurity. Interfaces are being simplified, notifications prioritized, and procedures redesigned to align with how people naturally think and act. By reducing friction, organizations encourage compliance without coercion.

Leadership plays a decisive role in shaping security behavior. Employees mirror the attitudes of their leaders. When executives demonstrate that cybersecurity is a business priority, teams follow suit. Conversely, when leadership treats security as a technical afterthought, it signals to staff that shortcuts are acceptable. Leaders who model good behavior such as using secure communication channels, reporting incidents promptly, and supporting awareness campaigns, create ripple effects across the organization.

Psychological safety is another essential factor. Employees must feel comfortable reporting mistakes or suspicious activity without fear of punishment. In many organizations, breaches go unreported because individuals fear blame or disciplinary action. A culture that emphasizes learning over punishment encourages early reporting, allowing incidents to be addressed before they escalate. This mindset requires trust and empathy from management, as well as clear policies that protect those who act responsibly.

The organizational structure itself influences cybersecurity outcomes. Centralized security models, where all decisions flow through a single department, may ensure consistency but can create bottlenecks. Decentralized models empower departments to make security decisions relevant to their context but risk inconsistency. The optimal approach blends both; centralized oversight with distributed responsibility. Each department should have security champions trained to interpret policy within their operational realities while remaining accountable to enterprise-wide standards.

Human resources also play a subtle yet vital role. From recruitment to exit processes, HR departments shape the lifecycle of access and accountability. Background checks, security clearances, onboarding education, and exit interviews all serve as control points for managing insider risk. Neglecting these steps can expose organizations to sabotage or data theft by disgruntled or departing employees. Integrating cybersecurity protocols into HR functions bridges the gap between technical and human management.

Social engineering remains one of the most persistent threats because it exploits trust and emotion rather than code or infrastructure. Phishing, pretexting, and impersonation attacks succeed by manipulating curiosity, urgency, or authority. Even highly trained employees can be deceived if an attacker convincingly mimics a trusted colleague or supplier. The defense against such manipulation lies in vigilance, verification, and collective awareness. Encouraging employees to question unusual requests, confirm identities, and share suspicious communications creates a human firewall as effective as any technological one.

Diversity and inclusion also contribute to stronger cybersecurity. Diverse teams bring varied perspectives, reducing blind spots in risk perception and decision-making. Gender diversity, cultural variety, and interdisciplinary collaboration enrich the collective intelligence of a security team. Different life experiences enable individuals to detect unconventional attack patterns and question assumptions that homogeneous teams might overlook. Inclusive cultures also foster psychological safety, encouraging open communication and collaborative problem-solving.

On an organizational level, cybersecurity maturity depends on alignment between departments. Security cannot exist in isolation from finance, operations, or marketing. Every decision ,from vendor selection to customer engagement carries security implications. Integrating cybersecurity into corporate governance ensures that it becomes part of every strategic conversation. When risk assessments, budgeting, and performance reviews all include security metrics, the organization embeds protection into its DNA.

Change management is another critical dimension. As technology and processes evolve, employees must adapt. Resistance to change often leads to security gaps, especially when new systems or policies are introduced without adequate explanation. Transparent communication and user-centered design can ease transitions. Employees should understand not just how to use new systems, but why those changes matter. Engagement in the process turns resistance into ownership.

Ultimately, cybersecurity is a social discipline disguised as a technical one. The most advanced defenses can be undone by one careless click, while the most modest tools can be made powerful by an alert and informed workforce. Protecting an organization's digital assets means protecting the people who interact with them through education, empathy, and empowerment.

Organizations that succeed in mastering the human and institutional dimensions of cybersecurity achieve more than protection; they cultivate resilience. They create environments where people act not out of fear but out of conviction, where compliance is not enforced but embraced, and where security becomes an instinct as natural as innovation. The result is not only safer systems but stronger organizations built on trust, unity, and shared responsibility.

Building a Human-Centered Security Culture

At the heart of every resilient enterprise lies culture, the collective mindset that shapes how people think, act, and respond to risk. A human-centered security culture recognizes that people are not liabilities to be controlled but assets to be empowered. Rather than viewing employees as the weakest link, organizations that adopt this perspective see them as the first line of defense.

Building such a culture begins with empathy and engagement. Employees must understand not only the rules but the reasons behind them. Security awareness campaigns often fail because they rely on fear rather than motivation. Telling employees that one mistake could cost the company millions might secure short-term compliance, but it rarely builds long-term commitment. A better approach connects security to shared values such as trust, innovation, and customer protection. When individuals perceive security as a means of preserving what they care about, their participation becomes genuine and consistent.

Storytelling is a powerful tool in this process. Sharing real-life examples of data breaches, both internal and external, helps employees visualize consequences and recognize patterns of behavior that lead to compromise. Success stories, where early reporting or vigilance prevented a potential attack, should also be celebrated publicly. These narratives transform abstract risks into tangible realities and reinforce the idea that security is everyone's achievement.

Inclusivity is another pillar of human-centered security. Every employee, regardless of role or department, must feel that their contribution matters. From the front desk to the boardroom, everyone interacts with digital systems that can either strengthen or weaken the organization's defenses. Inclusive engagement ensures that policies are designed with diverse perspectives in mind, preventing blind spots that arise when decisions are made in isolation by technical teams alone.

Visibility and accessibility further reinforce culture. Security teams should not be distant or intimidating entities that employee's approach only when in trouble. They should be visible partners who guide, educate, and listen. Hosting open security days, feedback sessions, and informal Q&A forums bridges the gap between technical specialists and the broader workforce. This accessibility fosters trust, encouraging people to report suspicious incidents without hesitation.

Finally, leadership consistency cements culture. When employees witness leaders practicing what they preach using secure communication, adhering to policies, and owning mistakes ,they internalize those behaviors. Culture is sustained not through slogans but through example. In a human-centered security culture, protection becomes instinctive, trust becomes mutual, and security becomes a natural part of the organizational rhythm.

Organizational Learning and Continuous Improvement

Cybersecurity is a living discipline. Threats evolve, technologies advance, and regulations shift. In this constantly changing environment, static knowledge quickly becomes obsolete. The organizations that endure are those that learn continuously, absorbing lessons from incidents, industry developments, and internal experiences, and converting them into actionable growth.

Organizational learning begins with reflection. After every security incident or audit, teams must analyze what happened, why it happened, and how future occurrences can be prevented. These reviews should go beyond technical failures to examine procedural gaps and behavioral patterns. Was the policy misunderstood? Was communication too slow? Were roles unclear? By addressing systemic causes rather than symptoms, organizations transform incidents into opportunities for advancement.

Knowledge sharing is essential for sustaining improvement. Information silos where insights remain confined within departments undermine progress. Establishing collaborative platforms, such as knowledge bases, internal webinars, or cross-departmental meetings, ensures that lessons reach everyone who needs them. When a finance team learns from an attempted phishing attack, that knowledge should inform the behavior of HR, procurement, and customer support as well. Shared intelligence prevents repetition of mistakes and reinforces institutional memory.

Mentorship and succession planning also contribute to continuous improvement. Cybersecurity expertise cannot depend on a few individuals. Organizations must invest in developing new talent through mentorship, certification programs, and rotational assignments. This not only strengthens internal capacity but also ensures continuity when experienced personnel move on. Knowledge retention becomes a structural advantage rather than a vulnerability.

Measurement is another cornerstone of improvement. What cannot be measured cannot be managed effectively. Establishing metrics for incident response times, training participation, policy compliance, and employee feedback provides objective evidence of progress. These metrics should not serve as punitive tools but as indicators of growth. When trends show improvement, they validate strategies; when they show decline, they prompt timely intervention.

Continuous improvement also depends on curiosity and adaptability. Cyber threats often emerge from unexpected directions, requiring flexible thinking and experimentation. Encouraging a mindset of inquiry where employees feel free to question processes and suggest enhancements, turns the workforce into a dynamic learning organism. Regular innovation sprints or "security hackathons" can invite teams to brainstorm creative solutions to persistent challenges.

Finally, learning must be embedded into governance. The outcomes of lessons learned should feed back into policy, training, and investment decisions. An organization that institutionalizes learning transforms resilience from a reactive process into a proactive strategy. Over time, this iterative cycle creates a culture where mistakes are not feared but studied, where growth is continuous, and where the organization evolves faster than the threats it faces.

CHAPTER 10

The Future of Fraud Detection and Enterprise Resilience

The future of cybersecurity will not be defined by technology alone, but by the wisdom with which it is applied. As digital ecosystems become more integrated and intelligent, the line between opportunity and vulnerability grows thinner. Fraud detection and enterprise resilience are entering a new era where predictive insight, automation, and ethical governance must coexist in harmony. Organizations that understand this balance will thrive; those that neglect it will struggle to survive in a world where trust has become the ultimate currency.

Fraud detection in the next decade will depend heavily on predictive and adaptive intelligence. Artificial Intelligence will evolve from a tool of detection to one of anticipation. Rather than waiting for suspicious activity, systems will analyze behavioral trends, transaction histories, and external threat data to forecast potential fraud scenarios before they materialize. Machine learning models will learn not just from internal datasets but from global threat intelligence networks, creating a collective defense ecosystem. Financial institutions, insurance providers, and digital commerce platforms will share anonymized data to improve mutual protection, forming what experts call collaborative intelligence for fraud prevention.

Automation will also take center stage in future resilience. The combination of AI, robotic process automation, and smart orchestration tools will allow organizations to respond to threats in seconds. Incident containment, log analysis, and system restoration will increasingly rely on self-healing architectures. Systems will be able to isolate infected nodes, reconfigure network parameters, and restore clean versions of data autonomously. These capabilities will not eliminate the role of human professionals, but will redefine it, freeing people to focus on governance, innovation, and ethical oversight rather than repetitive operations.

However, the power of automation and intelligence brings a parallel challenge: the risk of hypercomplexity. As systems grow more interconnected, their dependencies multiply. A single misconfiguration in one component can cascade across entire networks. The more intelligent the system, the greater the potential for errors if oversight is weak. Future cybersecurity will therefore require simplified complexity; architectures that remain transparent, explainable, and governable. Designing security systems that are intelligent yet auditable will be essential to maintaining trust in both technology and the institutions that deploy it.

The evolution of fraud detection will also demand a reimagined approach to data privacy. The growing use of behavioral analytics and biometric identifiers, while powerful, raises questions about surveillance and consent. Enterprises must find ways to secure data without overstepping ethical boundaries. Privacy-preserving technologies such as differential privacy, secure multiparty computation, and federated learning offer promising solutions. These methods allow collaborative learning and detection without exposing raw user data. In the future, the best cybersecurity systems will not be those that know the most about people, but those that protect them while knowing the least.

Quantum computing represents another frontier. While still in its early stages, its implications for encryption and decryption are immense. Quantum computers will eventually be capable of breaking many classical encryption algorithms, rendering traditional security methods obsolete. To stay ahead, enterprises must invest in quantum-safe encryption and transition to cryptographic algorithms resistant to quantum attacks. The migration to post-quantum security standards will not be optional, it will be a prerequisite for continued trust in digital transactions.

Blockchain technology will play a growing role in maintaining data integrity. Its decentralized nature allows tamper-evident logging of transactions, providing transparent audit trails for fraud detection and compliance. Smart contracts; self-executing agreements coded directly onto blockchain networks can automate verification processes, reducing opportunities for manipulation. However, as blockchain adoption expands, new vulnerabilities will emerge, particularly through coding errors and integration flaws. The future will demand blockchain governance frameworks that balance immutability with adaptability.

Resilience, in the enterprise context, will evolve from recovery to anticipation. Future organizations will not only prepare for crises but design their systems to adapt automatically. Business continuity will no longer mean returning to normal; it will mean continuously redefining what normal looks like in a shifting environment. This mindset requires agility, cross-disciplinary collaboration, and investment in foresight. Cybersecurity teams will need to integrate closely with risk management, operations, and strategy functions to align resilience with business transformation.

Ethics and governance will become the guiding compass of this evolution. As cybersecurity becomes more automated, questions of accountability will grow. Who is responsible when an AI system makes a wrong decision? How do organizations ensure fairness when algorithms influence financial access or compliance enforcement? To navigate these challenges, enterprises will need ethics councils and governance boards that oversee the design, deployment, and monitoring of intelligent security systems. Transparency, explainability, and accountability will shape the public's trust in future digital infrastructure.

Education and skill development will define the human side of resilience. The cybersecurity workforce of tomorrow must combine technical mastery with strategic awareness and emotional intelligence. Professionals will need to understand not only how systems work but why people behave as they do. Interdisciplinary education, merging psychology, computer science, law, and management will become the norm. Organizations that invest in upskilling and continuous learning will maintain agility amid rapid technological change.

Global cooperation will also define the next chapter of enterprise resilience. Cyber threats transcend borders, and no organization or nation can defend alone. International coalitions focused on cyber diplomacy, information sharing, and capacity building will shape a more unified digital defense posture. Regional frameworks such as the African Union's cybersecurity initiatives and global ones like the Budapest Convention will evolve into binding agreements that encourage shared responsibility. Collaboration between public and private sectors will be indispensable to addressing emerging risks such as cyber warfare, deepfake fraud, and AI-generated misinformation.

Ultimately, the future of fraud detection and resilience rests on a single principle: adaptability. The threats of tomorrow will not resemble those of today. Technology will change, attack vectors will evolve, and risk landscapes will shift. The organizations that endure will be those that cultivate the ability to learn faster than adversaries, respond with integrity, and innovate with conscience.

In the coming years, resilience will no longer be measured by how well systems withstand attacks, but by how seamlessly they adapt and recover. Cybersecurity will become not just a technical discipline but a defining element of organizational character, a reflection of how responsibly enterprises harness power, protect trust, and pursue progress. The future belongs to those who understand that technology may defend systems, but people and principles defend societies.

REVIEWS

1. Dr. Aisha Abubakar

Director of ICT Policy and Innovation, National Information Technology Development Agency (NITDA)

"This book is both a technical guide and a strategic compass for cybersecurity professionals in Africa. Olakojo Kolawole Adebowale brings clarity to complex issues that have long challenged enterprise systems; fraud detection, payment security, and database resilience. What stands out most is the book's contextual relevance; it doesn't just copy global standards but adapts them to local realities. Every chapter builds on the next, helping professionals understand how to design systems that are secure by structure, not just by intention. This work will remain an essential reference for policymakers and enterprise security architects alike."

2. Engr. Ifeanyi Oduah

Cybersecurity Research Lead, Lagos Digital Security Forum

"Few books manage to bridge theory and application as effectively as Cybersecurity Principles for Fraud Detection. Kolawole Adebowale writes not just as an expert but as a practitioner who has seen

systems fail and fixed them. His insights into fraud detection, AI-powered defense, and Oracle database protection are grounded in reality. I particularly appreciate his attention to enterprise adaptability, how organizations can evolve from reactive defense to proactive resilience. This book deserves a place in every cybersecurity professional's library."

3. Mrs. Kemi Ogundele

Head of Risk and Compliance, SterlingPay Nigeria Ltd.

"As someone deeply involved in financial compliance and payment system governance, I found this book remarkably practical. It connects fraud prevention directly to the human and procedural aspects of financial technology, reminding us that systems are only as strong as the people managing them. Olakojo Kolawole Adebowale's treatment of secure payment infrastructures, real-time risk analytics, and fraud detection frameworks provides exactly what fintech operators need today: actionable knowledge. His approach is both structured and visionary, and I will be recommending this to every risk management team I work with."

4. Dr. Chidi Umeh

Senior Lecturer, Department of Computer Science, University of Lagos (UNILAG)

"This book is the missing bridge between academia and industry. It blends solid technical frameworks with case studies that reflect real-world complexity. For graduate students and researchers, it offers a modern roadmap for understanding enterprise cybersecurity ,from system deployment to database integrity. For professionals, it's a hands-on guide that turns abstract principles into actionable design. Kolawole Adebowale's command of both theory and implementation makes this book a cornerstone for anyone teaching or studying cybersecurity in Africa."

5. Mr. Daniel Omoyeni

Chief Executive Officer, Secure Path Technologies

"Having worked in enterprise security for over a decade, I can confidently say this book captures the core of what makes cybersecurity effective, clarity, structure, and accountability. Kolawole Adebowale's writing is grounded in experience, not abstraction. His emphasis on database security, fraud analytics, and secure payment architecture reflects a practitioner's mindset ,one focused on measurable results. The case studies, especially those on AI-driven fraud detection, demonstrate both innovation and practicality. This is more than a textbook, it's a professional manual for building cybersecurity maturity in any organization

REFERENCES

Aldasoro, I., Gambacorta, L., Giudici, P., & Leach, T. (2023). The role of big data and machine learning in cyber risk measurement. *Journal of Banking & Finance, 152*, 106821. https://doi.org/10.1016/j.jbankfin.2023.106821

Almorsy, M., Grundy, J., & Müller, I. (2021). An analysis of the cloud computing security problem. *ACM Computing Surveys, 54*(3), 1–37. https://doi.org/10.1145/3446375

Bada, A., Sasse, M. A., & Nurse, J. R. (2019). Cyber security awareness campaigns: Why do they fail to change behavior? *Cybersecurity, 2*(1), 29–37. https://doi.org/10.1186/s42400-019-0031-8

Böhme, R., Christin, N., Edelman, B., & Moore, T. (2015). Bitcoin: Economics, technology, and governance. *Journal of Economic Perspectives, 29*(2), 213–238. https://doi.org/10.1257/jep.29.2.213

Carter, L., & Belanger, F. (2022). The cybersecurity workforce gap and challenges in information security training. *Computers & Security, 120*, 102769. https://doi.org/10.1016/j.cose.2022.102769

Cheng, L., Li, Y., Li, W., Holm, E., & Zhai, Q. (2021). Understanding the violation of IS security policy in organizations: An integrated model based on social control and deterrence theory. *Computers & Security, 105*, 102241. https://doi.org/10.1016/j.cose.2021.102241

European Union Agency for Cybersecurity (ENISA). (2023). *Threat Landscape 2023: Trends and emerging threats.* https://www.enisa.europa.eu/topics/threat-risk-management/threats-and-trends

Feng, Y., Liu, W., & Liang, H. (2022). AI-driven fraud detection in digital finance: A comprehensive review. *Information Systems Frontiers, 24*(2), 473–488. https://doi.org/10.1007/s10796-021-10106-1

Hassan, H., Ismail, Z., & Rahman, M. (2020). Enhancing database security in cloud environments through encryption and key management. *International Journal of Information Management, 54*, 102164. https://doi.org/10.1016/j.ijinfomgt.2020.102164

Kraemer, S., Carayon, P., & Clem, J. (2009). Human and organizational factors in computer and information security: Pathways to vulnerabilities. *Computers & Security, 28*(7), 509–520. https://doi.org/10.1016/j.cose.2009.04.006

National Institute of Standards and Technology (NIST). (2018). *Framework for improving critical infrastructure cybersecurity (Version 1.1).* U.S. Department of Commerce. https://doi.org/10.6028/NIST.CSWP.04162018

Nguyen, T., Luo, X. R., & Hoang, D. (2023). The evolution of cybersecurity governance: Toward a framework for adaptive enterprise defense. *MIS Quarterly Executive, 22*(1), 37–55.

Pahi, D., & Yilmazel, O. (2023). Artificial intelligence in fraud detection: Balancing innovation, ethics, and data privacy. *Journal of Financial Crime, 30*(4), 1234–1251. https://doi.org/10.1108/JFC-06-2022-0129

Raj, R., & Dey, L. (2022). Quantum-safe cryptography: Securing data in the post-quantum era. *IEEE Access, 10,* 91345–91361. https://doi.org/10.1109/ACCESS.2022.3198425

Rezaei, A., & Dowlatshahi, M. (2021). A hybrid model for secure digital payment systems using blockchain and AI. *Journal of Network and Computer Applications, 182,* 103051. https://doi.org/10.1016/j.jnca.2021.103051

Salahdine, F., & Kaabouch, N. (2019). Social engineering attacks: A survey. *Future Internet, 11*(4), 89. https://doi.org/10.3390/fi11040089

Sarker, I. H., Kayes, A. S. M., & Watters, P. (2021). Cybersecurity data science: An overview from machine learning perspective. *Journal of Big Data, 8*(1), 13. https://doi.org/10.1186/s40537-021-00412-9

Shameli-Sendi, A., Aghababaei-Barzegar, R., & Cheriet, M. (2020). Taxonomy of information security risk assessment (ISRA). *Computers & Security, 88*, 101636. https://doi.org/10.1016/j.cose.2019.101636

Torelli, R., & Majumdar, S. (2021). Resilience by design: Integrating cybersecurity into enterprise strategy. *Journal of Business Strategy, 42*(5), 33–42. https://doi.org/10.1108/JBS-02-2020-0027

Vasiljeva, T., & Kochetkova, E. (2020). Ethical implications of AI in fraud detection systems. *AI & Society, 35*(3), 671–681. https://doi.org/10.1007/s00146-019-00884-4

Wang, L., Lin, P., & Yang, C. (2022). Enterprise cyber resilience: Governance, compliance, and recovery integration. *Computers in Industry, 136*, 103599. https://doi.org/10.1016/j.compind.2021.103599

Zhang, H., & Tang, J. (2023). Human-centered cybersecurity governance in financial technology ecosystems. *Journal of Information Security and Applications, 75*, 103503. https://doi.org/10.1016/j.jisa.2023.103503

www.ingramcontent.com/pod-product-compliance
Lightning Source LLC
Chambersburg PA
CBHW021215250926
51852CB00006B/21
* 9 7 8 4 7 0 6 2 4 6 2 8 3 *